Minimum Wages and On-the-Job Training

Minimum Wages and On-the-Job Training

Masanori Hashimoto

American Enterprise Institute for Public Policy Research
Washington and London

Masanori Hashimoto is associate professor of economics and public affairs at the University of Washington, Seattle.

Library of Congress Cataloging in Publication Data

Hashimoto, Masanori.
    Minimum wages and on-the-job training.

    (AEI studies ; 311)
    Bibliography: p.
    1. Wages—Minimum wage.   2. Employees, Training of.
I. Title.   II. Series.
HD4917.H38   331.2′3   81-1435
                                 AACR2
ISBN 0-8447-3428-4

AEI Studies 311

Printed in the United States of America

Contents

LIST OF TABLES

LIST OF FIGURES

Preface

One of the most serious effects of minimum-wage legislation is the impairment of on-the-job training (OJT) for young workers. Consisting of many kinds of learning through experience as well as formal training programs, OJT provides young workers with basic skills, stimulates their motivation, nurtures their sense of responsibility, and generally cultivates attitudes conducive to productivity in work. By creating a barrier to OJT, minimum wages may cause serious harm to their future labor-market experience.

The primary purpose of this monograph is to formulate a theoretical argument and to present empirical evidence on the effects of minimum wages on OJT. According to my findings, minimum-wage legislation forces young workers to forgo some OJT and in effect to bargain away some of their future earnings in exchange for a small increase in their current wages. The prospect that minimum-wage legislation will discourage OJT raises serious doubts about the law's wisdom, especially concerning its application to young workers.

Chapter 1 casts this research into perspective by briefly reviewing recent evidence on minimum-wage effects, by discussing some new directions in research, and by presenting some relevant background on the labor-market history of young workers. Chapter 2 presents an analytical framework appropriate for the analysis of how OJT affects earnings and discusses some empirical evidence on the relevance of this framework to reality. In chapter 3, I formulate a theoretical model of a competitive labor market and analyze how such a market determines the mix of current wage and OJT. I then analyze the manner in which minimum wages affect both this mix and employment. In chapter 4, I use the model to measure the effects on OJT of the 1967 amendments to the Fair Labor Standards Act, which involved a major expansion of coverage as well as an increase in the minimum wage. I then discuss my findings based on this model and offer additional evidence and insights culled from the literature. Chapter 5 offers summary discussions and some policy implications.

I wish to express my gratitude to the following individuals and institutions for their valuable support: Yoram Barzel and Keith Leffler for their incisive comments, which deepened the theoretical analysis in chapter 3; Shoichi Ito, Levis Kochin, and Jacob Mincer for stimulating discussions at various points; Richard Elmore for bringing to my attention the *New York Times* article cited in chapter 1; Barbara L. Brugman for her constructive comments, which improved the entire draft; Shoichi Ito and Prapan Tianwattanatada for competent and reliable research assistance; Marian Bolan for expert typing; Simon Rottenberg (the project director of the AEI Minimum Wage Project) and Thomas F. Johnson (director of Economic Policy Studies at AEI) for encouragement and generous support; and the College of Arts and Sciences and the Graduate School of Public Affairs, both at the University of Washington, for computer-related resources. Without their help, I doubt if this monograph would have seen the light of day. Any remaining errors are my own responsibility.

1
Background Discussions

The State of the Knowledge about Minimum-Wage Effects

After months of congressional squabble against a history of judicial opposition, the federal minimum wage, along with other employment-related provisions of the Fair Labor Standards Act (FLSA), was finally enacted in October 1938.[1] By 1980, the minimum-wage provisions had been amended six times, most recently in 1977, the level of the nominal minimum rising with each amendment and major expansions of the coverage taking place in 1961, 1967, and 1974.

Table 1 shows the persistent upward trend and widening scope of the federal minimum-wage law. Clearly, the most notable change has occurred in coverage. Although the basic minimum wage relative to the average manufacturing wage has fluctuated around the 50 percent mark, the coverage almost doubled between 1938 and 1980. As column 3 of the table indicates, the federal minimum wage now covers almost 84 percent of the nonsupervisory labor force. Column 4 presents a standard measure of the effective minimum wage calculated as the product of columns 2 and 3. This measure incorporates both the relative size of the basic minimum wage and the extent of coverage. It shows a persistent upward trend over time, and by January 1981 the effective minimum wage will have increased by 140 percent since October 1938. As for the future prospect, coverage is likely to continue expanding, and attention may increasingly be directed toward

[1] For an informative historical sketch of the evolution of the minimum-wage law, see Jonathan Grossman, "Fair Labor Standards Act of 1938: Maximum Struggle for a Minimum Wage," *Monthly Labor Review*, vol. 101 (June 1978), pp. 22-30. Welch presents a useful synopsis of changes in the minimum-wage provisions. See Finis Welch, *Minimum Wages: Issues and Evidence* (Washington, D.C.: American Enterprise Institute, 1978), chap. 1.

TABLE 1
The Basic Minimum Wage and Aggregate Coverage, 1938–1981

Month/Year of Change in Minimum Wage	Basic Minimum Wage Changed to (dollars) (1)	Basic Minimum Wage as a Percentage of Average (straight-time) Manufacturing Wage (2)	Percent Coverage of All Nonsupervisory Employees in Private Nonagricultural Work (3)	Effective Minimum Wage [(2) × (3)]/100 (4)
October 1938	0.25	41.7	43.4	18.1
October 1939	0.30	49.5	47.1	23.3
October 1945	0.40	42.1	55.4	23.3
January 1950	0.75	54.0	53.4	28.8
March 1956	1.00	52.9	53.1	28.1
September 1961	1.15	51.2	62.1	31.8
September 1963	1.25	52.7	62.1	32.7
February 1967	1.40	51.5	75.3	38.8
February 1968	1.60	55.6	72.6	40.4
May 1974	2.00	47.2	83.7	39.5
January 1975	2.10	45.1	83.3	37.6
January 1976	2.30	46.0	83.0	38.2
January 1978	2.65	48.4	83.8	40.6
January 1979	2.90	49.7	83.8	41.6
January 1980	3.10	49.9	83.8	41.8
January 1981	3.35	51.9	83.8	43.5

SOURCE: Columns 1 through 3 are from Welch, *Minimum Wages*, table 1.

raising the rate of compliance with the law.[2] The prospect that the scope of the minimum-wage law will continue to widen adds urgency to the need to evaluate the effects produced by the law.

The primary intent of the law is clearly to reduce poverty among low-skilled workers. Economists have long been concerned with the possibility that the law produces undesirable side effects. They are especially concerned with the possibility that the adverse effects fall primarily on the young and the low-skilled, the very labor groups that the law is intended to protect. Much of the recently accumulated evidence tends to bear out the validity of such concerns. For sound evaluations and informed policy discussions of the law, one can ill afford to ignore the evidence that has accumulated about its adverse effects.

Most of the studies undertaken by economists have aimed at assessing the effects of the minimum wage on employment and unemployment rates. The theory of employment and unemployment effects of minimum wages is a straightforward application of elementary demand-supply analysis. An effective minimum-wage law, by definition, raises the wage rate in the covered sector above its level in the absence of the law. Since labor becomes more expensive than before, employers reduce the quantity of labor services they purchase, a phenomenon resulting in disemployment effects. The consequent reduction in the employment demand leads to some unemployment in the covered sector. The minimum wage may also attract workers to the covered sector to look for employment at the increased wage, thereby adding to the unemployment effect. Of course, a precise analysis must take into account the fact that the reduced probability of finding a job in the covered sector will counteract the effect of the increased wage on the incentive to look for employment there. Also, one might expect unemployment to disappear eventually, as

[2] Both noncompliance and noncoverage evidently are important phenomena, especially among very-low-wage workers. Gramlich reports that in 1975 the minimum-wage law raised the wage of only about half of all low-wage workers. See Edward M. Gramlich, "Impact of Minimum Wages on Other Wages, Employment, and Family Incomes," *Brookings Papers on Economic Activity*, no. 2 (Washington, D.C., 1976), pp. 409-61. Ashenfelter and Smith estimate that for the United States as a whole the compliance rate was about 69 percent in 1973. See Orley Ashenfelter and Robert Smith, "Compliance with the Minimum Wage Law," *Journal of Political Economy*, vol. 87, no. 2 (April 1979), pp. 333-50. The extent of noncompliance is likely to be greater if employers have less room to adjust in the total compensation package offered to workers. As we shall see in chapter 2, a compensation package typically contains various fringe benefits, opportunities for on-the-job training, etc., in addition to wages. Thus employers may comply with the law but may respond to an increased minimum wage simply by reducing these nonwage payments.

3

those workers not finding employment in the covered sector move to noncovered sectors or to activities outside the labor force. In a dynamic economy in which the inflow of new workers to, and outflow of old workers from, labor markets are pervasive, however, unemployment effects tend to persist as long as the minimum wage remains effective. Since these effects are greater the higher the minimum wage relative to the wages that would prevail in the absence of the law, they are most likely to be felt by low-skilled workers.

Past studies by and large confirm the prediction that higher minimum wages reduce employment opportunities and raise unemployment, particularly for teenagers, minorities, and other low-skilled workers. The reader is referred to a recent monograph by Welch, which offers a comprehensive treatment of the current state of knowledge about minimum-wage effects.[3] In addition, a study by Moore, which Welch does not discuss, is of some interest to us.[4] Moore estimates separately the effects of expanded coverage and the effects of the basic minimum wage on the unemployment rate of teenagers and young adults. His findings indicate, as expected, large unemployment effects exerted by both coverage and the basic minimum wage on teenagers' unemployment rates. According to his findings, the effects tend to diminish as youths reach the twenty- to twenty-four-year-old group. By then, their wage is likely to have increased above the minimum. Generally, measured unemployment effects are greater for nonwhites than for whites.

The minimum wage has also significantly reduced the availability of full-time jobs for teenagers.[5] Evidently, teenage workers tend to be sorted into part-time jobs, which typically pay lower wages than full-time jobs. As we shall see in chapter 4, increased part-time jobs may reflect increased school enrollments as a result of minimum wages. Part-time work is an important method of financing education for many youths. It may also signify a reduction in on-the-job training

[3] Welch, *Minimum Wages.* For some illuminating discussions of the policy relevance of some of the past studies, see Robert Goldfarb, "The Policy Content of Quantitative Minimum Wage Research," *Industrial Relations Research Association Proceedings* (1974), pp. 261-68. Recently, Brown, Gilroy, and Kohen have surveyed the literature on minimum-wage effects on youth employment and unemployment for the Minimum Wage Study Commission. See Charles Brown, Curtis Gilroy, and Andrew Kohen, *Effects of the Minimum Wage on Youth Employment and Unemployment,* Minimum Wage Study Commission Working Paper, no. 1 (Washington, D.C., 1980).

[4] Thomas Gale Moore, "The Effects of Minimum Wages on Teenage Unemployment Rates," *Journal of Political Economy,* vol. 79, no. 4 (July/August 1971), pp. 897-902.

[5] Gramlich, "Impact of Minimum Wages," pp. 442-43.

(OJT), for part-time jobs are likely to offer less OJT than full-time jobs. In addition, observers have noted adverse minimum-wage effects on the labor force participation rate—the proportion of a specific population that is either employed or unemployed. A 1970 study by Hashimoto and Mincer, as well as the recent study by Ragan, documents the sequence of effects, from increased minimum wages to reduced employment opportunities and, eventually, reduced labor force participation.[6] These effects were observed to be more pronounced among low-wage groups. Evidently, many marginal workers sooner or later drop out of the labor force altogether rather than wait in the queue of the unemployed to find a job paying the minimum wage.

The preceding discussions refer to minimum-wage effects on employment and unemployment. There are also important minimum-wage effects on the stability of employment. Over the course of fluctuating economic activities, marginal workers often tend to experience unstable employment. Basically, this phenomenon reflects employers' attempts to adjust labor costs to changing economic conditions without having to incur the high fixed costs that are involved in altering the employment of physical capital and skilled workers. Thus when labor demand rises, employers expand labor inputs first by increasing the overtime for the existing work force and by expanding the employment of low-wage workers before adding to the skilled employees. When demand drops, they contract labor inputs by letting go of the low-wage workers first as well as by reducing overtime. Note that employers could adjust labor costs in response to changing demand by altering wage rates. Such a strategy would help reduce their total reliance on employment as an adjustment mode. For marginal workers, however, such wage adjustments may have to occur around the minimum wage. An effective minimum wage represents a floor below which the employers cannot cut wages. As a result, firms are forced to use employment reduction as an adjustment mode.

[6] Masanori Hashimoto and Jacob Mincer, "Employment and Unemployment Effects of Minimum Wages," mimeographed (Washington, D.C.: National Bureau of Economic Research, 1970); and James Ragan, "Minimum Wages and Youth Labor Market," *Review of Economics and Statistics*, vol. 59, no. 2 (May 1977), pp. 129-36. Labor force withdrawal obviously lessens the minimum-wage impacts on the *measured* unemployment rate, for the measured unemployment is defined as the number of persons unemployed divided by the sum of those employed and unemployed. Mincer discusses a model using the probabilistic nature of job search to address this and other, related phenomena. See Jacob Mincer, "Unemployment Effects of Minimum Wages," *Journal of Political Economy*, vol. 84, no. 4, part 2 (August 1976), pp. S87-S104.

The definitive work on this issue is by Kosters and Welch.[7] They find that between 1954 and 1968, a typical teenage worker was more than four times as likely as a typical adult worker to lose a job during a downturn in economic activity. The minimum-wage hikes during these years, according to their study, seem to have reduced the cyclical employment variability of white adult males by about one-third but to have more than doubled teenage employment variability. Although it has long been recognized that teenagers and other low-skilled workers suffer from cyclical instability of employment, the recent evidence on the role of the minimum wage in promoting these workers' employment instability is a matter of added concern.

Finally, the following excerpts from a recent *New York Times* article offer direct evidence bearing on minimum-wage effects on the employment opportunities of young workers. Referring to an unpublished report by the United States Department of Labor, Shabecoff writes:

> The survey found that a majority of the young people would be willing to take low-paying jobs in such areas as fast-food restaurants, cleaning establishments, supermarkets as well as dishwashing. A substantial number of the young people surveyed said they would work at below the minimum wage.
>
> The survey suggests that the younger the worker the lower the wage and level job he is willing to accept. It also indicated that young minority group workers will take lower level work than young white people.[8]

These findings conform perfectly to the predictions based on an elementary economic logic.

The preceding brief discussion reveals that the minimum-wage law reduces employment opportunities for low-skilled workers, increases their unemployment as well as their withdrawals from the labor force, and reduces their employment stability in the course of the inevitable fluctuations in economic activity. The results of these studies indicate, therefore, that the minimum-wage legislation is inconsistent with the policies of enhancing job opportunities for low-skilled workers. To be sure, one may quibble with the precise

---

[7] Marvin Kosters and Finis Welch, "The Effects of Minimum Wages on the Distribution of Changes in Aggregate Employment," *American Economic Review*, vol. 62, no. 3 (June 1972), pp. 323-32.

[8] Phillip Shabecoff, "U.S. Finds Big Jobless Rate in Youth Ranks," *New York Times*, February 29, 1980. The U.S. Department of Labor report is based on the findings from a recent National Longitudinal Survey.

magnitudes of the effects or may complain about the inconclusiveness of some of the findings. It would be very difficult, however, to offer enough counterevidence to undermine the general consensus to which the existing evidence points.

New Directions in Studies of Minimum-Wage Effects

Research interests recently have shifted increasingly toward topics other than the traditional employment and unemployment effects. It is recognized, for example, that minimum wages may reduce fringe benefits received by covered workers.[9] Faced with an increased wage mandated by the law, employers may counter by cutting back on various nonwage payments, including flexibility in hours of work, pleasant work environment, job safety, and on-the-job training. Extending the notion that minimum wages encourage labor force withdrawals, some investigators have analyzed the effects on enrollment in school, a major alternative use of time for many young workers. The argument is that a minimum-wage-induced increase in unemployment lowers the opportunity cost of attending school while increasing the payoff to schooling, the completion of which is likely to lead to jobs with wages greater than the minimum wage. Evidence from recent studies indicates that minimum wages do indeed reduce fringe benefits and increase school enrollments of teenagers.[10] In chapter 4, we shall relate the significance of these findings to our own in some detail.

My main concern in this monograph is one component of fringe benefits. Although fringe benefits include such standard amenities as pleasant working environment, inexpensive insurance, and job safety, perhaps the most important fringe benefit for young workers is the opportunity that jobs offer to acquire new skills and knowledge and to improve on the old. Such opportunity is referred to as on-the-job training and is essential to enhancing the future productivity and earning capacity of young workers. Although jobs undoubtedly differ in both the quantity and quality of OJT they offer, learning processes, associated with both formal training programs and informal learning

---

[9] Mixon's, to my knowledge, is one of the first empirical studies of the effects on fringe benefits. See Wilson Mixon, "Some Economic Effects of Minimum Wage Legislation" (Ph.D. diss., University of Washington, 1974). At this writing, Lazear, Leighton and Mincer, and Wessels are studying minimum-wage effects on the formation of human capital and on fringe benefits. See chapter 4 of this monograph for results of some of these studies.

[10] Findings by Ehrenberg and Marcus, Cunningham, and also Mattila on school-enrollment rate will be discussed in chapter 4.

by experience, are believed to be the basic characteristics of practically all working activities.

A growing number of scholars concerned with the problems of the youth labor market recognize the importance of OJT in ensuring future labor-market success of young workers. For example, many authors identify the lack of OJT as a main cause of the plight of black workers. In a recent issue of *Scientific American*, Eli Ginzberg makes the following forthright observation:

> A disproportionately large number of young blacks are having serious and prolonged difficulties gaining a foothold in the world of work. What is worse is that many of those who encounter serious difficulties in their formative years (from 16 through 24) fail to acquire the experience, training, competences and credentials that would earn them a regular job yielding a reasonable income in their adult years.[11]

Surprisingly, Ginzberg does not acknowledge the role that minimum-wage laws play in creating this unfavorable phenomenon for minority workers. In fact, a few paragraphs earlier he simply dismisses the possibility that the minimum-wage law affects youth labor markets to any significant degree.[12] The minimum-wage law, however, does impair OJT in at least two ways. First, by reducing employment opportunities, the law blocks the access to OJT for affected workers. Second, even if some workers remain employed at the minimum wage, their employers may respond to the increased minimum wage by cutting back on the formal training programs or simply by reducing the quality of working environments necessary to stimulate learning.

The proposition that minimum wages may have long-lasting impacts on young workers through their effects on OJT has been advanced by a number of scholars. The following commentaries by three reputable economists succinctly state this proposition. In discussing his hypothesis that individuals learn from their working experiences, Sherwin Rosen suggests that

> the effect of a minimum wage is to put a ceiling on the range of learning opportunities to workers. . . . [As a result, their] range of choice is severely constrained and guarantees a relatively flat life-time income pattern.[13]

[11] Eli Ginzberg, "Youth Unemployment," *Scientific American*, vol. 242, no. 5 (May 1980), pp. 43-49.

[12] "The only thing one can say for the minimum wage in this context [the unemployment problem] is that it has not been helpful to some small number of young job seekers" (Ginzberg, "Youth Unemployment," p. 40).

[13] Sherwin Rosen, "Learning and Experience in the Labor Market," *Journal of Human Resources*, vol. 7, no. 3 (Summer 1972), pp. 326-42, at pp. 338-39.

8

In his essay on unemployment problems in the United States, Martin Feldstein states that

> the minimum wage law has an unambiguously harmful effect on some young workers. Even if an individual were willing to "buy" on-the-job training by taking a very low wage for six months or a year, the minimum wage law would not permit him to do so. . . . For the disadvantaged, the minimum wage law may have the ironic effect of lowering lifetime incomes by a very large amount.[14]

Finally, writing generally on minimum-wage issues, Finis Welch observes:

> These benefits, which range from opportunities for on-the-job training or a pleasant work environment to health and disability benefits, are affected [by minimum wages] because they can be substituted for wages. . . . Since workers can take the benefits of training with them when they leave for other employment, firms may have little incentive to offer training. But . . . they can offer on-the-job training in exchange for lower wages . . . a wage floor impedes this trade-off: as wages are forced upward, employers have fewer incentives to accommodate learners.[15]

Note that these remarks refer to the harmful minimum-wage effects that fall on *employed* workers. Although the logical basis for the proposition is unquestioned, there has been little evidence presented to support its validity. Researchers are now attempting to fill this gap. How important is OJT to a typical young worker? Have minimum wages impeded OJT differently for white and black persons? Are the increases in current wages that minimum wages confer on some workers large enough to compensate for the reduced future earnings caused by the curtailment of OJT? In subsequent chapters, I develop evidence bearing on these and other, related questions.

Labor Force Participation, Employment, and Unemployment of Young Workers

Since our interest is focused primarily on the minimum-wage effects on young workers, it is useful to have some background knowledge about the labor-market history of this category of workers. Figures 1 and 2 depict the post–World War II trends in the labor-market

[14] Martin Feldstein, "The Economics of the New Unemployment," *Public Interest*, vol. 33 (Fall 1973), pp. 3-42, at p. 15.
[15] Finis Welch, "The Rising Impact of Minimum Wages," *Regulation* (November/December 1978), pp. 28-37, at pp. 31-32.

9

FIGURE 1
Trends in Labor-Market Experience of Young Males

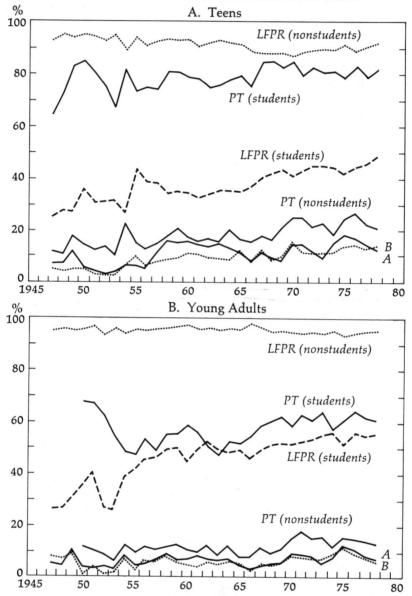

NOTE: LFPR = labor force participation rate. PT = percentage of employed workers who are in part-time jobs. A = unemployment rate for nonstudents. B = unemployment rate for students.

SOURCE: U.S. Department of Commerce, Census Bureau, *Current Population Survey* (October of every year depicted).

FIGURE 2
Trends in Labor-Market Experience of Young Females

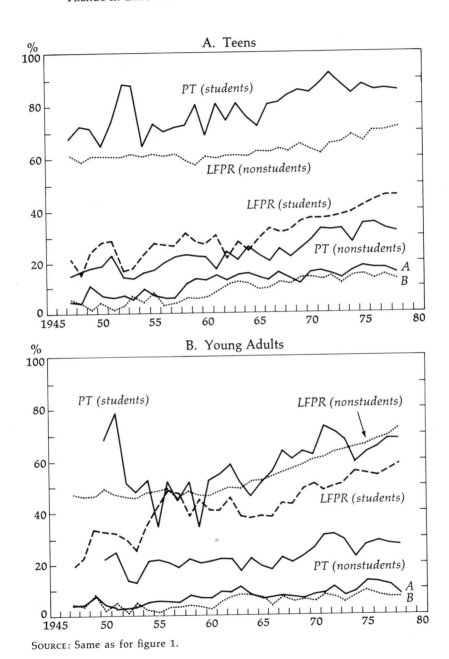

SOURCE: Same as for figure 1.

experience of young workers.[16] In these figures, "teens" refers to postsecondary youths of eighteen and nineteen years of age. "Young adults" refers to individuals twenty through twenty-four years of age. In examining these figures, it is useful to recall the general trend in the school-enrollment rate (not depicted in the figures). For both male teens and male young adults, the school-enrollment rate—the proportion of the population that is enrolled in school—showed a steady upward trend until the end of the 1960s. In the early 1970s, the school-enrollment rate started to decline for males, a phenomenon commonly attributed to the depression in the rate of return to schooling. The enrollment rate stayed depressed through 1977. Being in school is by no means a dominant occupation for males, especially for young adult males. In October 1978, 49 percent of male teenagers and 70 percent of male young adults were not enrolled in school. These youths were mostly in the labor force. For females, the upward trends in the school-enrollment rate were sharper than for males throughout the entire period and did not show the same declining trend in the 1970s. One reason for the continued upward trend in female enrollment is the expanding employment opportunities for educated females in the 1970s. Still, being in school is not the predominant occupation for female youths. In October of 1978, a little more than 56 percent of female teens and about 80 percent of female young adults were neither attending school nor serving in the military.

The labor force participation rate (LFPR), not surprisingly, is much higher for nonstudents than for students. More noteworthy is the substantial difference that still remains in the LFPR between male and female nonstudents despite some narrowing during the past two decades. For male nonstudents, the LFPR fluctuates around 90 percent or higher, but for female nonstudents it has reached only about 60 percent in recent years. Quite clearly, labor markets provide the primary areas of activities for male nonstudents and, increasingly, for the majority of female nonstudents. One obvious reason for the persistently lower female LFPR is that homemaking is still an important occupation for young women.

Most employed students work at part-time jobs, while employed nonstudents are found predominantly in full-time jobs.[17] Note that the proportion of employed persons working in part-time jobs has been rising over time for both students and nonstudents. The general

[16] The data for these figures were kindly provided by Professor J. Peter Mattila, who used them for his analysis of school enrollment effects, discussed in chapter 4. The data refer to October of each year.

[17] Part-time workers are those working fewer than thirty-five hours during the survey week.

upward trend for the proportion of employed nonstudents in part-time jobs is of particular relevance for our study, for part-time jobs are likely to offer less on-the-job training and fringe benefits than full-time jobs.

The figures also show the trends in the unemployment rate for these labor groups. There is a slight upward trend in the unemployment rate, and it is greater for teens than for young adults. Also, although there is a tendency for the unemployment rate to be higher for students than for nonstudents, the difference is rather small, and the ranking is sometimes reversed. These findings suggest that youth unemployment has to do more with such features as race, urban-rural residence, and minimum wages than with school-enrollment status.

Finally, it should be noted that teenagers and young adults are by no means the dominant labor group among the low-wage earners. Both Gramlich and Welch discuss this point in detail using the Current Population Survey data.[18] Gramlich reports that only about one-third of those earning less than $2.00 in 1973, when the minimum wage was $1.60, were teenagers. Half of the total low-wage earners were part-time workers, and a little more than one-fourth were heads of families. According to Welch, about two-thirds of the low-wage labor group were female, one-tenth were more than sixty-five years of age, and almost one-half were twenty-five to sixty-four years of age. Clearly, the problems associated with low wages are not restricted to teenagers and young adults. My research, however, focuses on the possible harmful effects of the minimum-wage law on the formation of human capital through on-the-job training. For this issue the relevant groups to consider are teenagers and young adults, for whom on-the-job training is crucial in determining future earning capacity.

Some impression of the proportion of young workers whose on-the-job training may be affected by minimum wages can be inferred from the calculations performed by Welch. He estimates that in 1975, when the minimum wage was $2.10 per hour, 51.4 percent of teenage wage earners (sixteen to nineteen years of age) and 23.8 percent of young adult wage earners (twenty to twenty-four) earned hourly wages between $2.00 and $2.49.[19] These figures indicate that a sizable share of young workers are employed at wages near the minimum wage. The issue to which the remainder of this monograph is devoted is to what extent the minimum-wage law affects their future earnings by impeding the provision of on-the-job training.

---

18 Gramlich, "Impact of Minimum Wages," table 12, and Welch, *Minimum Wages*, chap. 2.

19 Welch, *Minimum Wages*, table 5.

2
How On-the-Job Training Increases Earnings

To examine how minimum wages affect the amount of on-the-job training provided to workers, it is instructive to discuss OJT first within the broad conceptual framework of the standard human capital analysis. This discussion clarifies the process of increasing earnings through training and facilitates the analysis of how the minimum-wage law impinges on this process.

What is human capital? Included in the notion of human capital are skills, experience, useful information, good health, personal contacts, and other productivity-enhancing attributes that are embedded in a person. These attributes are assets, or capital, because they are acquired at costs, and their benefits in increased productivity accrue over time. In this respect, these attributes resemble machines and other physical capital. Unlike machines, however, it is impossible in a nonslave society to sell one's human capital to someone else. Being inseparable from the person who owns it, human capital is distinct from physical capital. Broadly conceived, any worker owns some human capital. More experienced, more knowledgeable persons have more human capital than others. These persons are generally more productive and earn higher incomes than others. It is often claimed that by far the most important asset a typical person owns is his human capital, not physical properties, stocks, or bonds.

Schooling and OJT are the two primary avenues for acquiring human capital. Unlike schooling, however, OJT is difficult to observe. By its nature, much of skill acquisition takes place as part of work experience, making it difficult to distinguish between time spent on learning and time spent purely on work. Even with formal training programs, the paucity of relevant data on resources devoted to such programs precludes a direct measurement of the magnitude of OJT.

The theory discussed in this and the following two chapters is designed to overcome this difficulty.

Consider a youth who enters the labor market at a particular time. In the ordinary course of events, his earnings grow as he accumulates years of work experience. Inflation aside, the general increase in his labor productivity is the primary source of such wage growth. According to the human capital theory of earnings and the empirical evidence that has been offered to support it, an important factor in the growth of earnings, especially for young workers, is on-the-job training (OJT). As discussed in the previous chapter, the concept of OJT refers to employment activities that offer a worker the opportunity to acquire skills, information, knowledge, and other human capital that enhance his future productivity. Just as relevant is the quality of the work environment that stimulates his motivation for productive efforts, develops his sense of responsibility, and cultivates his general attitudes toward work. By viewing OJT broadly to include all job-related opportunities that enhance a worker's future market performance, economists have gained a greater understanding of the relationship between work experience and earnings. Although some jobs offer OJT through a formal training program, many jobs require little or no formal training program. The absence of a formal training program does not preclude the possibility that the worker acquires human capital on the job.[1] A learning-by-experience process still takes place in these jobs through informal instruction, observations, experimentation, etc. An inexperienced worker, for example, may be permitted during working hours to observe skilled workers operate complicated equipment. He may even be allowed to operate it himself at times. Such opportunities are clearly invaluable in enabling the worker to acquire useful knowledge.

On-the-job training, then, is a process of investment in human capital. Such investments entail costs, which arise directly through the use of skilled manpower and machines for the purpose of "instruction," as well as through the provision of work environments conducive to learning. More indirectly, these costs arise as inexperienced workers waste raw materials, produce defective outputs, and cause additional wear and tear on machines and equipment. Offsetting these costs are benefits that accrue either to the worker or to the employer or to both. Benefits accrue to the worker in the form of increased

---

1 See, for example, Jacob Mincer, *Schooling, Experience, and Earnings* (New York: National Bureau of Economic Research, 1974); and Edward Lazear, "Age, Experience, and Wage Growth," *American Economic Review*, vol. 66 (September 1976), pp. 548-58.

earning power, and they accrue to the employer in the increased productivity of his capital that the trained worker helps realize.

How are the costs and the returns split between the employer and the worker? The answer to this question hinges on the important conceptual distinction between general and specific on-the-job training [2] and is central to this analysis of minimum-wage effects on OJT. If the training creates only general skills, which increase the worker's productivity in other firms as well as in the firm providing the training, the worker must bear the entire costs. The reasoning is as follows. The employer would be willing to bear the costs only if he were assured that the worker would continue to stay with him after the training is completed. But the worker would have no reason to prefer this employer to others after the training is completed, since his value is increased equally in this and in other firms. Unless the employer could enslave the worker, he would have no assurance that the worker would stay with him, and he would have no incentive to pay any part of the training costs. On the other hand, the worker has every incentive to bear the costs because he can take the skills anywhere. Therefore, the worker pays the costs and receives the entire return from the investment. He pays the costs implicitly by forgoing part of his earning capacity. Although explicit payments were common in nineteenth-century apprenticeship, modern practices are characterized predominantly by implicit payments. [3]

Besides general skills, training may create specific skills, which increase the worker's productivity more in this than in other firms. In this case, neither the employer nor the worker has the incentive to bear all the costs. Suppose that the employer bears all the costs. He must then expect to collect all the returns. If the worker receives no benefits from the investment, however, he will be indifferent to a choice between staying in this firm and taking another job. The employer, then, has no assurance that the worker will stay with him. Faced with the prospect of a capital loss caused by the worker's quitting, the employer has no incentive to enter into such a commitment.

[2] The theory was originally formulated in Gary S. Becker, "Investment in Human Capital: A Theoretical Analysis," *Journal of Political Economy*, vol. 70, supplement (October 1962), pp. 9-49. See Masanori Hashimoto, "Firm-Specific Human Capital as a Shared Investment," *American Economic Review* (in press), for some elaborations and formalization of the theory.

[3] High transaction costs of explicit payments may be one reason for the prevalence of implicit pricing. For example, with explicit payments the employer may have to maintain records of payments for income tax purposes. Moreover, the worker may be unable to deduct explicit payments from income taxes if OJT is provided in an informal setting. See a related discussion in Sherwin Rosen, "Learning and Experience in the Labor Market," *Journal of Human Resources*, vol. 7, no. 3 (Summer 1972), pp. 326-42.

FIGURE 3
Relationship between Training and Earnings

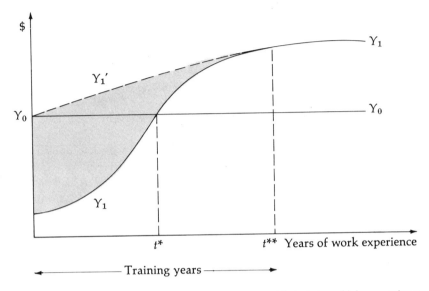

NOTE: Y_0 = no-training earnings. Y_1 = earnings with training. Y_1' = earnings capacity during training.

SOURCE: Author.

Similarly, the worker will have no incentive to pay all the costs and to collect all the returns because the employer, who will have no stake in this worker, will then be indifferent to a choice between keeping him and replacing him with a new worker. The solution is to share the costs and the returns. By sharing the investment, the parties create the incentive to stay together so as not to lose the benefits of the investment.

The preceding discussion reveals that the worker pays some or all of the costs of training, depending on how generally applicable the resulting skills are. A typical relationship between training and earnings is portrayed in figure 3. This figure focuses on training as the sole factor responsible for the growth of earnings. Thus, no training means that earnings stay the same. This is clearly an abstraction from reality, in which multitudes of influences—the general growth of the economy, inflation, luck, physical and mental strength, etc.—shape the course of earnings over one's life cycle. This abstraction is useful for the type of analysis we are interested in, however, and it does not distort the substance of conclusions derived from the analysis as long as training and other influences are largely independent of one

17

another. In figure 3, the horizontal line, Y_0, represents the earning schedule that a worker would have if there were no training involved. This no-training earning schedule indicates that his earnings are the same year after year because, to simplify the analysis, other influences on the shape of the experience-earnings profile are not taken into account.

The schedule Y_1 depicts the earning profile when there is some OJT in early years of employment. Earnings in early years are lower than the no-training earnings, reflecting the fact that the worker bears some of the costs of the training by accepting earnings that are lower than they would be if no training were provided. Earnings grow as learning accumulates and eventually overtake Y_0 as OJT decreases and the worker continues to collect returns on the accumulated investments. It is worth noting that the investment does not end at the overtaking time, t^*. Rather, the investment continues until time t^{**}. Before t^{**} this worker's earning capacity is constantly growing, as indicated by the dotted line Y_1', reflecting the ever-accumulating potentially recoupable returns—full earning capacity—to the previous investments. But the worker continues to forgo some of the recoupable returns by receiving Y_1 (which is smaller than the full earning capacity, Y_1', in each year). In fact, the entire shaded area represents the worker's payments for training in the form of forgone earnings.

How relevant to reality is the theory just outlined? Basically, there are two approaches to assessing the theory's relevance. One may attempt to measure directly the magnitude of OJT involved for different occupations. Alternatively, one may look for plausible effects of OJT, even though one cannot directly observe the amount of OJT itself. This second approach is exactly analogous to verifying the existence of gravity—itself an invisible force—by seeing that an object falls at a certain speed under a given set of circumstances. In many situations, this second approach is quite effective in demonstrating the validity and the usefulness of a theory. The existing literature offers fine examples of these two approaches, resulting in significant contributions to an understanding of a variety of labor-market phenomena. We now turn to some of these examples.

Widely recognized as one of the pioneers of the theory of training and of human capital in general, Mincer was the first researcher systematically to document the importance of OJT investments in the American economy.[4] He used earnings profiles like those in figure 3 to calculate the costs of schooling and of OJT for 1939, 1949, and

[4] Jacob Mincer, "On-the-Job Training, Costs, Returns, and Some Implications," *Journal of Political Economy*, vol. 70, supplement (October 1962), pp. 50-79.

TABLE 2

AGGREGATE ANNUAL INVESTMENT IN TRAINING AT SCHOOL
AND ON THE JOB: U.S. MALES, BY LEVEL OF SCHOOLING, 1958

Educational Level	Investments (billions of dollars)		
	School	Job	Total
College	8.7	8.7	17.4
High school	8.4	3.8	12.2
Elementary	4.5	1.0	5.5
All levels	21.6	13.5	35.1

SOURCE: Mincer, "On-the-Job Training," table 2.

1958. To save space, the details of his methodology will not be presented here; he essentially calculated the magnitude of the shaded area in figure 3. Since the substantive findings are similar for the three years, let us look at a summary of findings for 1958. According to table 2, OJT amounts to 38 percent of the combined schooling and OJT investments in 1958. For college-educated workers, the share of OJT is 50 percent. Clearly investments in OJT are just as important as schooling investments in the overall process of skill formation in the economy. According to Mincer, the accumulation of annual costs of OJT investments continues well past age forty, the annual amount of investments gradually declining with age. Although many scholars, including Mincer himself, have subsequently explored the implications of OJT for the shapes of earnings profiles, Mincer's research of 1962 remains a landmark study of this important issue.

Worth noting also is the study of Oi,[5] who was concerned with the phenomenon of OJT and its implications for layoffs. He cites International Harvester's study of the costs of employing a new worker. These are largely fixed and include, among other costs, those of recruiting, orientation, and unemployment compensation, as well as various training costs. They are fixed costs because they vary with the number of workers that the firm hires but not with hours of work. Oi's study indicates that in 1951 the training costs for the International Harvester Company, relative to the total fixed employment cost, not including workers' forgone earnings, were 22 percent for common labor, 98 percent for "two-year progressive students," and more than 99 percent for four-year apprenticeship.[6] Quite clearly, by far the most

[5] Walter W. Oi, "Labor as a Quasi-fixed Factor," *Journal of Political Economy*, vol. 70, no. 6 (December 1962), pp. 538-55.
[6] Oi, "Labor as a Quasi-fixed Factor," p. 546.

important component of the fixed costs of employment is training costs.

More recently, Lazear developed an imaginative econometric model to measure the OJT component of compensation received by young male workers.[7] Using a sample from the National Longitudinal Survey, he found that between 1966 and 1969 a typical white male who was fourteen to twenty-four years of age in 1966 received 40 percent of his total compensation in OJT. The proportion for a typical black male was 36 percent. In other words, a significant part of young men's annual salaries is paid in OJT, whose benefits accrue to these workers in increased future earnings. Incidentally, Lazear's study reveals an interesting trend in the early 1970s. He finds that white males gained in OJT more than did nonwhites, a widening gap occurring at the same time as the narrowing of the nonwhite-white wage gap. Indeed, his calculations indicate that apparent nonwhite gains in pecuniary wages between 1966 and 1974 were more than offset by declines in the OJT component of earnings. On balance, nonwhites became worse off relative to whites during the early 1970s. One possible cause for this phenomenon is the ever-rising minimum wage.

Recognition of the importance of OJT has contributed to the understanding of the shapes of earning profiles and of labor turnover. One important development is the human capital earning function. For example, Mincer demonstrates that by incorporating years of work experience with schooling attainment, one obtains sharper estimates of the rate of return to schooling and an increased understanding of the behavior of earnings over the life cycle of a typical worker.[8] He illuminates such issues as why earnings first rise with age and eventually decline and why the peak earnings are reached at different ages for different skill groups.[9]

The effects of OJT may be observed in labor turnover also. Here the emphasis is on firm-specific human capital. As noted earlier,

[7] Lazear, "Age, Experience"; and Edward Lazear, "The Narrowing of Black-White Wage Differential Is Illusory," *American Economic Review*, vol. 69 (September 1979), pp. 553-64.

[8] Mincer, *Schooling, Experience*.

[9] See also Yoram Ben-Porath, "The Production of Human Capital and the Life Cycle of Earnings," *Journal of Political Economy*, vol. 75 (August 1967), pp. 352-65. OJT appears to play important roles in Japanese markets. See Masatoshi Kuratani, "The Theory of Training, Earning, and Employment" (Ph.D. diss., Columbia University, 1973); Haruo Shimada, "The Structure of Earnings and Investments in Human Resources: A Comparison between the United States and Japan" (Ph.D. diss., University of Wisconsin–Madison, 1974); and Masanori Hashimoto, "Bonus Payments, On-the-Job Training, and Lifetime Employment in Japan," *Journal of Political Economy*, vol. 87, no. 5 (October 1979), pp. 1086-104.

when specific human capital is involved, both the employer and the worker have the incentive to share the costs and returns of the investments. This incentive stems from their mutual desire to reduce costly future separations. Thus, specific human capital creates a kind of voluntary binding contract that gives each party an incentive to avoid costly separations. If the amount of specific human capital increases with the skill level of the worker, one would expect turnover to be smaller for more skilled workers. Most recent studies, many of which are discussed in an informative survey by Parsons, find evidence confirming the validity of this proposition.[10]

To be sure, the human capital theory is not the only theory that predicts a lower turnover rate for more skilled workers. It is well known that firms adjust to short-run fluctuations in demand by varying employment of variable factors of production, leaving the quantity of physical capital relatively unchanged. The traditional complementarity hypothesis asserts that skilled workers are complementary to physical capital. Therefore, to extract productivity from the steady employment of capital, firms must maintain an equally steady employment of skilled workers.[11] Note that this theory considers only the firms' incentive to minimize the labor turnover of skilled workers. Nothing is said about the workers' incentive to reduce quits. The human capital theory, on the other hand, predicts a reduction of both layoffs and quits as skill level increases.

The discussion in this chapter demonstrates the value of the analytical framework of OJT in enhancing our understanding of many labor-market phenomena. By recognizing that the costs of OJT are paid implicitly and that the subsequent returns accrue in increased earnings, the human capital analysis has helped to clarify many phenomena that were once puzzling. I now employ this conceptual framework to analyze how the minimum wage alters the process of the accumulation of human capital through OJT and how it affects future earnings.

[10] Donald O. Parsons, "Models of Labor Market Turnover: A Theoretical and Empirical Survey," *Research in Labor Economics*, vol. 1 (1977), pp. 185-223.
[11] For a rigorous formulation of this argument, see Sherwin Rosen, "Short-Run Employment Variation in Class-I Railroads in the United States," *Econometrica*, vol. 36 (July 1968), pp. 511-29. Rosen discusses both this and the human capital argument in this article.

3
How Minimum Wages Reduce On-the-Job Training

An effective minimum wage reduces the amount of OJT and deters the growth of young workers' earning capacity in two ways. First, to the extent that the minimum wage leads to reduced employment and to increased unemployment, it deprives affected workers of opportunities to acquire skills on the job. This is an obvious, long-lasting effect associated with the minimum wage–unemployment link discussed in chapter 1. Second, the minimum wage retards the growth of earning capacity by causing a reduction in the amounts of OJT provided to those who remain employed. The analysis here is concerned with this latter effect of minimum wages.

According to the discussion in chapter 2, workers pay for all of the general training and some of the specific training by receiving current wages that are lower than those they would receive if no OJT were offered. To comply with an increased minimum wage, employers must raise pecuniary wages for those workers who receive less than the minimum wage. Since an increased minimum wage itself does little to increase worker productivity, employers will respond to increased current wages by reducing the amounts of OJT and other fringe benefits they offer to these workers. Thus, current wages may increase for these workers, but subsequent growth in their wages will be depressed.

One may well wonder why an increased minimum wage might not induce an employer instead to increase OJT for some workers. After all, if he has to pay higher wages than before, why would the employer not have the incentive to increase the productivity of the affected workers? To see the fallacy in this reasoning, recall the distinction between general and specific human capital. For young workers, for whom training creates skills that are often generally applicable to many jobs, the employer lacks the assurance that the trained workers will stay with him. For such training to occur, the workers must bear the bulk of the training costs. The increased minimum wage prohibits many of these workers from paying for the training costs by forgoing part of their current wage, that is, by accepting wages lower than their actual earning capacity (see figure 3). Even if the skills created by the training are firm-specific, the difficulty still remains, because the increased minimum wage limits the extent to which the workers can share the costs of training.

Although the preceding arguments appear sensible, some questions remain unanswered. For example, what happens to the workers' full wage as minimum wages cause a reduction in OJT while increasing their pecuniary wages? Is it possible for the affected workers to be made better off by minimum wages? How do minimum wages affect the rate of employment when OJT is included in the analysis? To answer these questions, it is useful to examine the gist of these arguments in more detail. The analysis in chapter 2 was concerned with the relationship between training and the earnings of an individual worker. Here we are interested in what the relationship implies for the rate of current wages and the amount of OJT in a free competitive market and, more specifically, in how the minimum-wage law alters this mix. To keep the analysis simple, I ignore technical details that would detract from my main points.[1] The algebraic formulation of the crucial aspects of the model appears in appendix A.

It is reasonable to presume that a typical worker is indifferent, given a choice between one dollar of pecuniary wage received today and an amount of OJT that will give him a future income worth exactly one dollar in present value. Therefore, the worker's decision as to which employer he will work for is based on the sum, rather than the relative magnitudes, of current pecuniary wage and the value of OJT offered by the employer. I shall call this sum a full wage. Under this assumption, the supply curve of labor to this labor market depends on the full wage, as portrayed in figure 4. The supply curve is upward-sloping, indicating that the higher the full wage offered, the greater is the number of workers who are willing to offer labor services in this market. From this supply curve, it is possible to generate a family of supply curves that relate the number of workers to the current pecuniary wage (W). Along any one curve, the amount

[1] Barzel discusses a related model to analyze effects of measurement costs on economic organization. See Yoram Barzel, "Measurement Cost and the Economic Organization of Markets," manuscript (University of Washington, 1980).

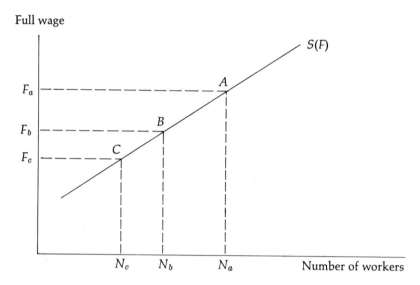

FIGURE 4
SUPPLY OF LABOR

Full wage

$S(F)$

F_a

A

F_b

B

F_c

C

N_c N_b N_a Number of workers

SOURCE: Author.

of OJT is fixed. In figure 5, $S(1)$ refers to the supply curve when one dollar's worth of OJT is provided, and $S(2)$ and $S(3)$ denote the supply curves corresponding, respectively, to two and three dollars' worth of OJT provided. The fact that the supply curve shifts to the right as OJT is increased simply means that given a pecuniary wage rate, more labor services will be supplied, the greater is the amount of OJT. The difference in the height between any two curves measures the difference in the *value* of OJT associated with each curve. Thus the height between $S(1)$ and $S(2)$ is one dollar, as is the height between $S(2)$ and $S(3)$. Figures 4 and 5 are simply two different ways of looking at the same phenomenon: the number of workers who are willing to work in this market increases as current wages or the amount of OJT or both are increased.

We now turn to the demand side of the analysis. As noted in chapter 2, providing OJT entails costs. If the skills acquired through OJT are general, the employer will "charge" the worker the costs of the training.[2] For young workers, skills and knowledge acquired on the job may have a general applicability to a wide variety of jobs, and

[2] If training is specific, the model applies to the portion of the training paid for by the worker.

FIGURE 5
Pecuniary Wage and Employment

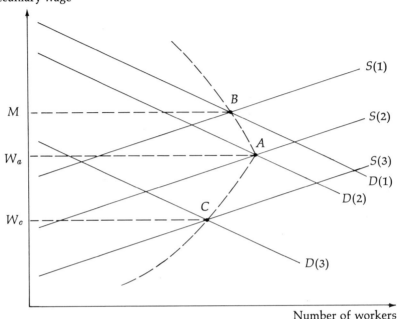

Pecuniary wage

M

W_a

W_c

B

A

C

S(1)

S(2)

S(3)

D(1)

D(2)

D(3)

Number of workers

Source: Author.

setting aside the issue of who pays the costs for the moment, it is reasonable that the marginal cost—an incremental total cost—of employing a worker rises as more OJT is provided to each worker. Put another way, hiring another worker becomes more costly as the job offers more OJT. Therefore, the employer is willing to pay less current pecuniary wage, for a work force of a given size, the more OJT is provided. As a result, the demand for labor as a function of the current pecuniary wage shifts down as OJT is increased. In figure 5, $D(1)$, $D(2)$, and $D(3)$ depict the demand curves, respectively, for one, two, and three dollars' worth of OJT provided. The demand curves are downward-sloping, indicating that given the amount of OJT, employers will buy a greater quantity of labor service, the lower the wage rate. It is worth pointing out that, unlike the supply curves, the difference in the height between any of these demand curves measures the difference in the marginal cost of employing another worker associated with each demand curve rather than the difference in the value of OJT provided. We assume that the marginal cost of employing another worker rises, or shifts upward, at an increasing rate as more OJT is provided.[3] Therefore, the distance between $D(2)$ and $D(3)$ is greater than that between $D(1)$ and $D(2)$.

The supply and demand curves, both functions of the current pecuniary wage, must be matched with each other for the same values of OJT. The dashed line in figure 5 traces the locus of the intersections of demand and supply curves for different values of OJT. A point on this line shows the number of workers, a current pecuniary wage, and the value of OJT, all three quantities that are consistent with one another—but which point on this dashed line will be chosen? To shed light on this question, we must recall a theorem in economics stating that in a free market based on voluntary exchange of goods and services, the sum of gains to all participants from such exchange will be maximized.[4]

In figure 6, the gains to the employers are depicted as the area a, and to the workers as the area b. To understand the meaning of areas a and b, think of the demand curve as the schedule of the employers' maximum wage offers for each additional worker. To obtain the employment level of E_{max}, the employers would be willing to pay the sum of the maximum wage offers for the set of successive workers. This sum is area a plus the wage bill, that is, a plus b plus c. Since competition among workers for jobs enables the employers to obtain the E_{max} level of employment by paying only b plus c, they receive area a as a bargain. Similarly, the supply curve is the schedule of the lowest wage that each additional worker will accept to work in this market. For E_{max} numbers of workers to work in this market, they would be willing to settle for a payment equal to area c. Competition among employers for their labor services results in their paying b plus c, however, giving the workers area b as a bargain. The key factor in this analysis is voluntary exchange in the presence of competition among employers for labor services and among workers for jobs.

The market equilibrium occurs when the sum of the areas a and b is the largest. In a simple case in which the demand curves are parallel to one another,[5] the equilibrium point corresponds to the point of the largest employment.[6] If the demand curves are not parallel, equilibrium occurs at less than the maximum employment. The analy-

---

[3] This assumption appears to be implicit in most discussions of the minimum-wage effects on OJT.

[4] Well-known exceptions are cases when a good being exchanged has spillover effects such as pollution or when the good is a public good such as police protection or television broadcasts.

[5] The supply curves are always parallel to one another by construction.

[6] See appendix A for an algebraic proof of this proposition.

FIGURE 6
Competitive Equilibrium at Maximum Employment

Pecuniary wage

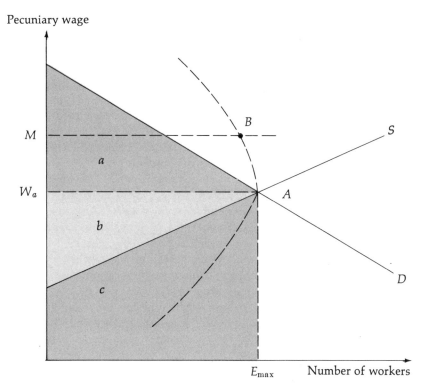

SOURCE: Author.

sis of minimum-wage effects on OJT will not be affected substantively either way.

In equilibrium the worker receives the pecuniary wage rate of W_a, which is smaller than what he would receive had the amounts of OJT been less. In effect, the worker pays implicitly for OJT by accepting a reduced current wage. Referring to figure 4, the equilibrium in the supply of workers occurs at the full wage of F_a, which equals W_a plus the value of OJT received.

How would a minimum wage affect this equilibrium? To answer this question, note that only the magnitude of the current pecuniary wage is controlled by the minimum wage, not the amounts of OJT or any other fringe benefits supplied on the job. Clearly, an imposition of a minimum wage (M) that is above the original equilibrium wage (W_a) will force a change in the equilibrium point, for example,

27

to B in figure 6. The prediction is straightforward. The minimum wage decreases both employment and the amounts of OJT. Since the gains both to the employers and to the workers are smaller at B than at the equilibrium point, A, the minimum wage causes a net loss to the employers and to the workers. As can be seen in figure 4, the lowering of the full wage results in a decrease in the rate of supply to this sector. Since some of the workers moving out of this sector will look for employment in the uncovered sector, the full wage in that sector will be depressed also. How the inflow of workers into the uncovered sector will affect OJT in that sector cannot be predicted readily from this model.[7]

Note that although the minimum wage may remain effective through time, it may not create long-run unemployment, or an excess supply of labor, in the conventional textbook sense. As long as the job package provides sufficient room for adjustment to the imposed minimum wage, no long-run unemployment occurs. Any unemployment that may occur is only temporary and is associated with those disemployed workers who are looking for work elsewhere.[8] Long-run unemployment will occur only when minimum-wage hikes are large enough so that OJT and other fringe benefits cannot be reduced sufficiently to offset them. In addition to the usual explanation relying on labor force withdrawals, these considerations may explain why researchers have often found ambiguous unemployment effects of minimum wages.[9]

Two elaborations are worth noting. First, as with most discussions on this topic in the literature, this analysis applies only when payments for OJT are made implicitly (workers receive a reduced current wage). This restriction does not detract from the generality of the analysis, however. As noted in chapter 2, modern practices are characterized predominantly by implicit payments. My analysis does imply, however, that increased minimum wages may lead to an increased use of explicit payments for the cost of OJT. For example, costs of some instructional materials, such as cassette tapes, notebooks, and raw materials—costs that previously were not charged—may be charged to the worker after minimum-wage hikes. Also, since em-

---

[7] See appendix A for further discussion.

[8] If information is costly, workers initially may believe that the minimum wage has caused the full wage to increase. As a result, short-run unemployment resulting from queueing may occur in the covered sector. This observation was offered to me by Jacob Mincer.

[9] Finis Welch, *Minimum Wages: Issues and Evidence* (Washington, D.C.: American Enterprise Institute, 1978), pp. 34-38. See also footnote 6 in chapter 1.

FIGURE 7
Competitive Equilibrium at Less Than Maximum Employment

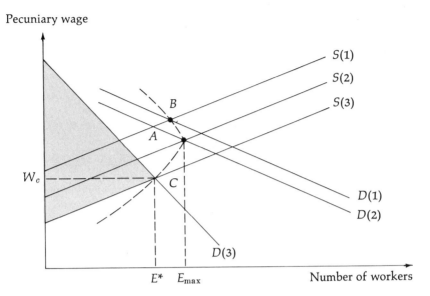

Source: Author.

ployers are unwilling to pay the cost of general training, the minimum-wage effect on OJT is expected to be more severe when general training is involved.

Second, my theory suggests a novel and somewhat surprising possibility. Suppose that the demand curves are not parallel to one another, as shown in figure 7. One reason why $D(3)$ is not parallel to $D(2)$ may be that the marginal cost of employment associated with a smaller amount of OJT rises less rapidly or even falls as employment is increased. This could occur, for example, if diseconomies of scale with employment are involved when larger amounts of OJT are provided. In this case, it is possible for a competitive equilibrium to occur at a point like C, where employment is less than maximum. An imposition of a minimum wage above W_c may *increase* employment, though the amount of OJT will definitely *decrease*. While the possibility that minimum wages will increase employment has been noted in the context of a monopsony market, the implication that employment may increase even in a competitive market is novel. It is clear from figure 4 that increased employment implies an increased full wage. Since the total gains from voluntary transactions must decrease, however, the employer must lose more than the worker gains.[10]

To summarize, minimum wages decrease the amount of OJT offered to some workers, even though these workers may remain employed. As a result, they decrease the gains from voluntary exchange in a competitive economy. This adverse consequence is likely to affect young workers the most, for OJT is crucial in determining their future labor-market experience. Other things equal, such an adverse effect is stronger the more general the skill created by OJT. For young workers, OJT is likely to lead to skills that are predominantly general and will earn them a regular job yielding a reasonably attractive income in their adult years. By curtailing opportunities to acquire these skills, minimum wages harm these workers' future labor-market potential, even though many of them enjoy an increased current wage without loss of their jobs.

---

[10] The employer is made to pay a lump-sum tax, as it were, while the marginal cost of employment is lowered. The reduced marginal cost in turn generates a force that increases employment. I owe this interpretation to Yoram Barzel.

4
Measuring Minimum-Wage Effects on Training

The analysis presented in chapter 3 indicates that effective minimum wages decrease the amount of OJT provided. One way of testing the validity of this prediction might be to "survey" relevant workers and their jobs and estimate the proportion of time spent on learning activities before and after an increase in the minimum wage. For example, before the minimum wage is raised, an inexperienced worker may spend a certain proportion of the day observing skilled workers handle complicated equipment and may even be permitted to operate it himself at times. According to my theory, after the minimum wage is raised, he will find the time spent on menial tasks increased and the proportion of time spent on learning decreased.

This direct approach is cumbersome, however, because the researcher must have a detailed knowledge about a job in order to be able to distinguish between activities that are an integral part of the job and those that constitute OJT. Classifying one activity as work and another as learning would, to some extent, be arbitrary and inaccurate. Also, surveys are costly to conduct. I am unaware of the existence of surveys that asked direct questions about the employers' response to increased minimum wages in the amount of on-the-job training they offer.[1]

An Empirical Model

My strategy is to infer minimum-wage effects from the experience-earnings profile. I ask how the minimum-wage law affects the job-experience-induced growth rate in an individual worker's earnings. Figure 8 conveniently summarizes the hypothesis under study. The

[1] See the "Discussion of Related Evidence" in this chapter for some survey evidence that is indirect.

FIGURE 8
Schematic Representation of Hypothesis

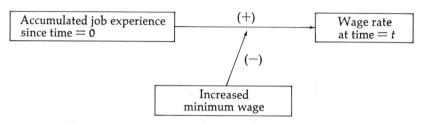

Source: Author.

arrow indicates the direction of causation, and the plus and minus signs indicate, respectively, whether the causation is positive or negative. The diagram states simply that the increased OJT through accumulated job experience raises the wage rate at some later time, t, but that the extent of this raise is attenuated by the minimum wage. What are the magnitudes of the positive and negative effects outlined in this diagram? How do these magnitudes differ for a white youth and a black one? The purpose of this chapter is to develop a simple empirical model that will enable us to answer these and other related questions.

To develop a useful model, one must first specify how job experience affects one's earning capacity. The starting point of this analysis is to express a typical individual's experience-earnings relationship in terms of observable variables. I first develop this relationship using simple algebra and then represent the basic model in figure 9. Suppose that this individual starts out with a wage rate of W_0 in year 0 but that his wage rate grows to W_t in year t. A simple way of expressing the relationship between W_0 and W_t is as follows:

$$W_t = W_0 + \delta W_0 \tag{1}$$

where δ is the rate of growth in the wage rate between the two years. My strategy is to see how various factors, including minimum wages, affect the value of the growth rate.[2]

The growth rate (δ) is hypothesized to be determined by the amount of OJT accumulated between the two years (ΔOJT), additional

[2] The logic of the strategy follows the model developed in Edward Lazear, "Age, Experience, and Wage Growth," *American Economic Review*, vol. 66 (September 1976), pp. 548-58.

FIGURE 9

SCHEMATIC REPRESENTATION OF MINIMUM-WAGE EFFECTS ON
ON-THE-JOB TRAINING

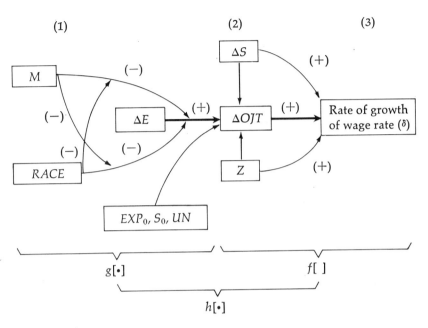

SOURCE: Author.

schooling obtained (ΔS), and a host of other factors (Z). The hypothesis is stated as follows:

$$\delta = f[\Delta OJT, \Delta S, Z] \qquad (2)$$

where $f[\bullet]$ is just a shorthand algebraic way of saying that the value of δ is determined by the three variables within the bracket. Although Z is treated here as a single variable to simplify exposition, it will in fact include a number of relevant control variables. These control variables are needed to hold constant the influences they represent. By including them in the equation, the relationship between δ and ΔOJT and ΔS can be more accurately measured. These control variables will be discussed in more detail later.

In the equation above, ΔS and Z can be calculated from available data, but not ΔOJT. Since OJT includes both formal and informal training, it cannot be accurately measured using available data. A standard approach in dealing with this type of situation is to specify

ΔOJT to depend on a group of observable variables. The selection of these variables is based on previous research reported in the literature. They include the accumulated work experience during the period (ΔE), a variable indicating whether the individual is black or white ($RACE$), the amount of work experience the individual had in the initial year (EXP_0), the initial level of schooling (S_0), and a variable indicating whether the individual is a union member or not (UN).[3] In addition, a minimum-wage index (M) is introduced as a variable so as to estimate the effect of the minimum wage on OJT. The relationship between ΔOJT and these variables can be expressed implicitly as:

$$\Delta OJT = g[\Delta E, RACE, EXP_0, S_0, UN, M] \qquad (3)$$

where $g[\cdot]$ denotes a functional relationship. The interaction among the variables ΔE, $RACE$, and M will be examined in order to determine how the minimum wage and the racial status of a person affect his job-experience-induced growth in OJT and earnings (see figure 9).

By substituting equation 3 in equation 2, it is now possible to express the rate of growth in the wage rate (δ) in terms only of observable variables, that is, in terms of ΔE, $RACE$, EXP_0, S_0, UN, M, ΔS, and Z:

$$\delta = h[\Delta E, RACE, EXP_0, S_0, UN, M, \Delta S, Z] \qquad (4)$$

where $h[\cdot]$ stands for a functional relationship. Once we estimate the parameters—coefficients—of function h, we will be in a position to assess how much the accumulated job experience increases the wage rate and, other things being equal, how minimum wages affect the link between accumulated job experience and the wage rate and how these magnitudes differ by race.

Figure 9 summarizes the empirical model just discussed. Columns 1 and 2 are linked by function $g[\cdot]$, columns 2 and 3 by function $f[\cdot]$, and columns 1, 2, and 3 by function $h[\cdot]$. As in figure 8, the plus and minus signs indicate whether the causation is positive or negative. These signs are indicated only for the relationships that are of immediate interest to this study. Note that both M and $RACE$ affect ΔOJT primarily through altering the relationship between ΔE and ΔOJT. In addition, $RACE$ exerts a negative impact on the already adverse effect of M on the relationship between ΔE and ΔOJT. These effects are the interaction effects noted earlier in the discussion of equation 3.

---

[3] The variable ΔE is constructed as the number of weeks worked during the period divided by 52. Thus it measures the proportion of a year spent at work. Since our main interest is in the variables ΔE, $RACE$, and M, to save space the rationale for including other variables and their predicted effects will not be discussed here. The interested reader may consult Lazear, "Age, Experience."

They simply mean that the adverse effect of minimum wages on training is greater for blacks than for whites.

The model outlined above will be used to calculate the value of OJT defined as follows:

$$OJT \equiv [\text{An increased hourly wage rate due to one}$$
$$\text{year's job experience}] \times [\text{the present value}$$
$$\text{of a stream of \$1 accruing every year from}$$
$$\text{now until retirement}] \qquad (5)$$

The second, present-value term appears because the increased earning capacity remains with the worker until he retires. As an illustration, suppose that the hourly wage rate for a twenty-year-old worker increases by \$0.30 as a result of this year's job experience. At a discount rate of 10 percent, a stream of \$1 accruing every year for the next forty-five years is worth \$9.86. Thus his increased earning capacity due to one year's job experience is worth \$2.96 (or \$0.30 $\times$ \$9.86). In other words, he is paid \$2.96 per hour in present-value worth of OJT in addition to his current money-wage rate. The sum of the money wage and the present value of OJT is the full wage (F), which was discussed in figure 4 in chapter 3. That is:

$$F \equiv W + OJT \qquad (6)$$

If this worker receives the money wage of \$2.00, his full wage is \$4.96. Minimum wages affect F through their effects on both W and OJT. According to my theory, although minimum wages may increase W, they definitely decrease OJT. Therefore, how a typical worker's full wage is affected depends on the relative strength of the positive effects on the wage and the negative effects on OJT. The net minimum-wage effects on the full wage, as well as effects on OJT, are assessed in the next section.

Before discussing the numerical estimates of minimum-wage effects, let us define the minimum-wage index (M) and the variables included in Z. A yearly minimum-wage index is assigned to each individual in the sample by adopting a standard formula as follows:[4]

$$M \equiv \left[\frac{\text{Applicable Nominal Minimum}}{\begin{array}{l}\text{(The individual's predicted wage}\\\text{in the absence of effective}\\\text{minimum wages)}\end{array}} \right] \begin{array}{l}[\text{probability}\\ \times \text{ of being}\\ \text{covered}]\end{array} \qquad (7)$$

[4] See appendix B for an elaboration of this calculation. The coverage information was obtained from U.S. Department of Labor, Employment Standards Administration, *Minimum Wage and Maximum Hour Standards under the Fair Labor Standards Act*, various issues between 1971 and 1977.

This definition follows the widely accepted notion that the expected impact of a minimum-wage law is greater, the higher is the applicable nominal minimum, the lower is the wage rate that the individual would receive in the absence of the law, and the greater is the probability that the individual will be covered. It might be suspected that in the regression analysis most of the explanatory power of the minimum-wage index originates in the denominator of M; that is, the primary source of the variability in the minimum-wage index may be the predicted wage rather than the nominal minimum or the probability of coverage. To guard against this suspicion, we include in the regression a variable ($\hat{W}$), which is the individual's predicted wage in the absence of the minimum-wage law.[5]

Among the variables included in Z are a dummy variable (MR_0), which is unity if the individual was married in the initial year and zero otherwise, changes in hours of work (ΔH), and age in the initial year (AGE_0). The choice of these particular sets of variables is guided by other studies of earnings in the literature.[6] These variables are included to control for influences other than those of the variables already discussed.

Evidence of Minimum-Wage Effects

In the previous section, I discussed the relationship between the rate of growth of earnings and several explanatory variables (see

[5] The predicted wage is calculated from an earnings function similar to that of Jacob Mincer, *Schooling, Experience, and Earnings* (New York: National Bureau of Economic Research, 1974), and estimated by using relevant information for 1966, one year before the change in the minimum-wage law. This approach assumes that the effective minimum wage was zero in 1966. This assumption is not unreasonable, for by 1966 the effectiveness of minimum wages had become eroded with the growth of labor productivity and inflation. Prior to 1966 the minimum wage was last increased in 1963. The earnings function relates the logarithm of 1966 hourly wage rate to schooling, years of work experience, a black-white dummy variable, a North-South dummy variable, and a set of twelve industrial dummy variables. The industries included are agriculture, mining, construction, manufacturing, transportation and communication, trade, finance-insurance-real estate, business and repair services, personal services, entertainment and recreational services, professional and related services, and public administration. The estimated earnings function is then used to predict wage rates in each year from 1967 to 1969. In calculating the predicted wage rates, we adjust the coefficients for the industrial dummy variables by the industry-specific growth rate of average earnings since 1966 to allow for the secular trend in the wage rate. See Masanori Hashimoto, "Minimum Wage and Earnings Growth of Young Male Workers," manuscript (University of Washington, 1981), for details.

[6] See, in particular, Edward Lazear, "The Narrowing of Black-White Wage Differential Is Illusory," *American Economic Review*, vol. 69 (September 1979), pp. 553-64.

equation 4). In this chapter I discuss the findings based on the statistical estimates of this relationship, paying particular attention to how minimum wages affect OJT.

Table 3 presents estimates of the relevant relationships based on the regression results that appear in appendix C. The regression number in table 3 corresponds to that in appendix C. These relationships tell how the minimum wage and other explanatory variables affect work-experience-induced growth in hourly earnings. As discussed earlier, the primary reason why work experience promotes growth in earnings is that an individual acquires OJT as he accumulates such experience.

The data used to estimate equation 4 were obtained using a sample of about nine hundred male workers fourteen to twenty-four years of age in 1966. This sample was drawn from the famous National Longitudinal Survey (NLS) and contains only those males who were not enrolled in school in either 1966 or 1969.[7] By examining these workers' wage growth between 1966 and 1969, we will assess the impact of minimum wages on the amounts of OJT and the full wage.[8] We consider the timing of this survey to be most fortunate in view of the significant increases in both the nominal minimum-wage rate and the coverage introduced by the 1967 amendments to the Fair Labor Standards Act. These amendments raised the basic minimum wage from $1.25 to $1.40 in February 1967 and to $1.60 in February 1968. They also involved a major extension of coverage to, among others, employees in large farms and in many private and public service establishments. As table 1 indicates, the coverage rate jumped from 62.1 percent in 1963 to more than 75 percent in 1967. The minimum wage for newly covered workers was set at $1.00 in February 1967 but was raised in a series of steps to $1.60 in February 1971.[9] I confine this study to males primarily because the labor

[7] The NLS is a multistage probability sample representing every state and the District of Columbia. The survey began in 1966, and the data are collected almost every year for the same cohorts of individuals. The focus of the survey is on a variety of economic, sociological, and psychological variables. The survey contains four subsets: middle-aged men who in 1966 were forty-five to fifty-nine years of age, women thirty to forty-four years of age, and young men and young women both between the ages of fourteen and twenty-four (subsets separated by sex). For details, see Herbert S. Parnes, "The National Longitudinal Surveys: New Vistas for Labor Market Research," *American Economic Review*, vol. 65, no. 2 (May 1975), pp. 244-49.

[8] Thus we shall be comparing wage rates before with those after the new minimum wage. Note that δ is approximated by $\ln W_{69} - \ln W_{66}$.

[9] U.S. Congress, *U.S. Code: Congressional and Administrative News*, no. 3, 95th Congress, 1st session, 1977, pp. 1245-53, 3201-61.

TABLE 3

WORK-EXPERIENCE-INDUCED GROWTH IN EARNINGS AS A FUNCTION OF MINIMUM-WAGE INDEX AND OTHER EXPLANATORY VARIABLES

Regression Number	Constant	M	UN	ΔS	$\hat{W}$	DUM	Estimates of $d\ln W_t/d\Delta E$ at the Means of Explanatory Variables
A sample of those with estimated 1969 hourly wage $\geq$ $1.60							
Whites: N = 651							
1	1.025 (2.98)	−1.020 (−2.81)	−0.156 (−1.20)	−0.164 (−2.08)	−0.130 (−1.40)	—	0.158 (2.44)
Blacks: N = 197							
2	−0.698 (−1.17)	0.388 (0.88)	−0.166 (−1.29)	−0.188 (−0.60)	0.189 (1.03)	—	−0.131 (1.30)

Entire sample with DUM = 1 if estimated 1969 hourly wage < $1.60

			Whites: N = 661				
3	0.573	−0.624	−0.601	−0.210	—	−0.001	0.102
	(3.52)	(−2.00)	(−3.63)	(−2.61)		(−2.77)	(2.98)
			Blacks: N = 226				
4	−0.050	0.066	f.o.	−0.584	—	−0.0005	−0.018
	(−0.24)	(0.21)		(−2.02)		(−1.23)	(1.31)

NOTE: Variable definitions: M = minimum-wage index; UN = union status in 1969; ΔS = additional schooling accumulated during 1966-1969; $\hat{W}$ = the denominator of the minimum-wage index; DUM = a dummy variable equaling one for a person whose estimated 1969 hourly wage rate is less than $1.60; — = not included; f.o. = forced out by the computer program because of multicollinearity. t-values appear in parentheses; t-values for $d\ln W_t/d\Delta E$ are square roots of the F-values.

SOURCE: These are estimates of $(d\ln W_t/d\Delta E)$ based on regression estimates reported in appendix C.

force participation rate is much higher for males than for females (see figure 1 in chapter 1). If the minimum wage has any effect on OJT, we should be able to observe it most among males. Also, because of my main interest in working males, I selected only the males who were not enrolled in school in either 1966 or 1969.

The regression estimates in table 3 indicate how the minimum-wage index and other explanatory variables affect the relation between the growth rate of earnings and the years of work experience. The estimates of the effects of the minimum wage on the earnings-experience relationship may possibly be overstated by including persons whose 1969 wage rates would have been less than the minimum wage in the absence of the law. To avoid this possibility, regressions 1 and 2 omit those whose 1969 wage would have been less than the minimum wage rate of $1.60 then prevailing, and regressions 3 and 4 use a dummy variable to control statistically for them within the multiple regression equation.[10]

Table 3 shows anomalous results for blacks. The last column of the table indicates that $d\ln W_t / d\Delta E$ is negative. This implies that additional work experience reduces earnings for blacks.[11] Although these results for blacks are not statistically significant—indeed, none of the regressions for blacks obtains significant F-values—I am still perplexed by the anomalous findings. The ambiguity of the black results may be due to the unlikely possibility that work experience actually reduces earnings for blacks or to the often encountered phenomenon that data are, for some unknown reason, less reliable for blacks than for whites. With the available information, it is impossible to determine which of these factors is important in explaining these results.[12] It is pertinent to note that researchers have often found ambiguous effects of minimum wages on the employment and unemployment experiences of blacks. Using the same data as mine, Ehrenberg and Marcus find ambiguous effects on school enrollments for

[10] The bias arises because the wage rates of those who would have earned less than the minimum wage rate in the absence of the law are raised by the law, thereby attenuating the experience effects on earnings as they are estimated by interpersonal comparisons. The hypothetical wage rate for 1969 was estimated by the same earnings function used to calculate the denominator of the minimum-wage index. It would be more accurate to identify individuals by whether they are affected by the newly covered rate ($1.30) or by the basic rate ($1.60), but the data do not permit such a distinction.

[11] Means and the standard deviations of the variables used to calculate $d\ln W_t / d\Delta E$ appear in appendix D.

[12] The small sample of blacks may be another reason for the ambiguous findings for blacks. In regressions using a combined sample, however, the anomalous results for blacks remain. For further details, see Hashimoto, "Minimum Wage and Earnings Growth."

nonwhites.[13] Anomalous findings for blacks in negative-income-tax experiments are also reported in the literature;[14] so, though disappointing, the inconclusive results in the black data come as no surprise.

In contrast to the ambiguous findings for blacks, the results for whites are quite revealing. Both regressions 1 and 3 are highly significant; F-values are, respectively, 4.13 and 4.66. The last column of the table indicates that an additional year of work experience increases the hourly wage rate of white males by 10 to 16 percent (in logs). These estimates are statistically significant at conventional standards. Note that in regression 3 DUM obtains a negative coefficient, indicating, as expected, that the measured effect of work experience on earnings is smaller for those whose wages would have been less than the minimum wage.[15]

Most relevant for this study are the statistically significant negative coefficients for the minimum-wage index (M). These coefficients indicate clearly that minimum wages indeed retard the rate of growth of earnings for young white males. I conclude that these findings are solid evidence confirming the validity of the hypothesis that the minimum wage decreases OJT.

To gain a quantitative sense of the minimum-wage effects, I have calculated the elasticities of OJT (η_{OJT}) and of the full wage (η_F) with respect to the minimum-wage index.[16] These elasticities measure the percentage changes in OJT and in the full wage that are induced by a 1 percent increase in the minimum-wage index. They are defined as follows:

$$\eta_{OJT} \equiv \frac{\text{percentage change in } OJT}{1 \text{ percent increase in } M} \tag{8}$$

and

$$\eta_F \equiv \frac{\text{percentage change in } F}{1 \text{ percent increase in } M} \tag{9}$$

---

[13] Ronald G. Ehrenberg and Alan J. Marcus, "Minimum Wage Legislation and the Educational Outcomes of Youths," *Research in Labor Economics*, in press.

[14] Albert Rees and Harold W. Watts, "An Overview of the Labor Supply Results," in Joseph A. Pechman and P. Michael Timpane, eds., *Work Incentives and Income Guarantees* (Washington, D.C.: Brookings Institution, 1975), pp. 60-87.

[15] See footnote 10. The variable DUM was interacted with the minimum-wage index and other variables, but a severe multicollinearity prevented the estimation of their coefficients. To focus attention on the minimum-wage variable, the results for explanatory variables other than the minimum-wage index are not discussed here.

[16] For the OJT calculations, I use a discount rate of 10 percent and forty-five years of working life.

Appendix E presents the method used in the elasticity calculations. For white males, I obtain the following estimates: using regression 1, η_{OJT} is calculated to be —2.71 and η_F to be —1.58; according to regression 3, η_{OJT} is —2.54, and η_F is —1.17. In other words, a typical young white male worker experiences a 2.5 to 2.7 percent reduction in OJT and a 1.2 to 1.6 percent reduction in the full wage as the minimum-wage index is raised by 1 percent.

Two cautions must be noted in interpreting these elasticities. First, I have implicitly assumed that OJT is the only fringe benefit relevant to young workers. While job-related learning may be the dominant fringe benefit, it is clearly an overstatement to say that it is the only one. To the extent that other fringe benefits exist in the compensation package and are less affected than OJT by the minimum wage, my estimates of the elasticity of the full wage overstate the true value.

The second note of caution has to do with the OJT elasticity. The evidence clearly indicates that, for young white males, the minimum wage reduces job-related learning and thereby flattens the experience-earnings profile. It is possible, however, that a typical youth affected by the minimum wage in one period will try to catch up for lost OJT in subsequent years when, simply because of aging, his productivity rises above the minimum wage, enabling him to purchase training. To the extent that such a catching up occurs, my estimates of the OJT elasticity overstate the true value.[17] On the other hand, it is possible that reduced learning in one period adversely affects learning in subsequent periods by decreasing the productivity of time spent in training during those periods.[18] Thus the worker suffering from reduced learning in one period continues to suffer from the decreased effectiveness of subsequent training and consequently from a slower accumulation of learning, even though the minimum wage is no longer relevant. To the extent that such cumulative-deficit effects exist, my estimates of the OJT elasticity understate the true value.

I have tried to determine which of these effects are important by estimating a relationship between the rate of growth of earnings

[17] Since an individual's remaining working life shortens as he ages, what was once a profitable investment in skills will become less profitable as he ages. For this reason alone, a complete catching up is not expected to occur.

[18] This argument is similar to the controversial "critical periods" hypothesis found in the animal psychology literature. Evidently the applicability of this hypothesis to learning by human youths has not been ascertained. For several papers on the critical-periods hypothesis, see John Paul Scott, ed., *Critical Periods* (Stroudsburg, Pa.: Dowden, Hutchinson and Ross, 1978).

during the 1969–1971 period and the minimum-wage index for the 1967–1969 period, holding other explanatory variables constant. If the catching-up effects are dominant, the minimum-wage index for the earlier period, 1967–1969, should positively affect the rate of earnings growth in the subsequent period, 1969–1971. If the cumulative-deficit effects are dominant, however, the minimum-wage index should negatively affect the subsequent rate of growth of earnings. In a variety of regression specifications, the minimum-wage index consistently obtained significantly negative coefficients, suggesting that the cumulative-deficit effects are dominant. Evidently, the adverse effects of minimum-wage laws on learning on the job persist in subsequent years.[19]

What would have been the average values of OJT and the full wage per hour in 1969 for young white males if the minimum-wage law had remained as it was in 1966? By using the 1966 value of the minimum-wage index, the hypothetical OJT is calculated to be $6.57 from regression 1 and $3.15 from regression 3. The hypothetical full wage turns out to be $10.03 and $6.58, respectively (compare equations 5 and 6).[20] These regressions yield an actual OJT in 1969 of $4.84 and $2.18, respectively, and an actual full wage of $8.32 and $5.64. These calculations assume a discount rate of 10 percent and forty-five years of remaining working life. Of course, the results will change with different discount rates and years of working life. Taken at face value, these calculations imply that the 1967 revisions in the minimum-wage law reduced the value of OJT for young white males by some 26 to 31 percent and the full wage by 14 to 17 percent, both being reflected as reduced earning power in 1969.

To summarize, the findings for white males confirm that minimum wages tend to cause reduced earnings growth through their adverse effects on job-related learning. Such adverse effects appear to persist for the youth even after his productivity rises above the minimum-wage level. The findings for blacks are inconclusive. They do not even support the basic notion that work experience enhances earnings.

[19] For regression estimates bearing on this issue, see Hashimoto, "Minimum Wage and Earnings Growth."

[20] These numbers are the averages of OJT and the full wage values calculated for each individual in the sample by applying the regression parameters to his values of explanatory variables. Although the estimates of OJT and the full wage vary considerably, the elasticities discussed earlier are rather stable between the two regressions. For methodological details for these calculations and related findings, see Hashimoto, "Minimum Wage and Earnings Growth."

Discussion of Related Evidence

It appears that the minimum-wage hikes that started in 1967 had substantial adverse effects on the value of OJT for young white male workers. Any offsetting increases in the current pecuniary wage were too small to compensate for the reduced value of OJT provided. As a result, these workers' full wages were substantially reduced.

My findings may be compared with those of the study by Leighton and Mincer.[21] Using the same NLS data analyzed in this study, they find adverse minimum-wage effects on the dollar wage growth to be statistically significant only for whites. The black coefficients are negative but largely insignificant. My findings also are more definitive for whites than for blacks. Although the minimum-wage variable and the regression specifications differ in this study and that of Leighton and Mincer, the findings are rather similar. Moreover, their other and more direct evidence corroborates my findings. Using the NLS data, they find minimum wages to reduce the amount of *formal* training for both white and black youths. Their results indicate that the effect is slightly stronger for blacks than for whites. This finding, however, is of limited value because it pertains only to formal training. They also calculate effects using data from the Michigan Income Dynamics Panel. These data contain the answer to a question asked in 1976: "Do you feel you are learning things on your job that could lead to a better job or to a promotion?" They find that the probability of an individual's answering in the affirmative decreases as his minimum-wage index is increased. They report only the results for white male workers, including adults, during the 1973–1975 period. These three sets of findings by Leighton and Mincer clearly corroborate my findings of adverse minimum-wage effects on OJT.

Although a survey approach to measuring minimum-wage effects on OJT entails some difficulties, the results of one survey on minimum-wage effects on fringe benefits in general are worth noting here. Wessels discusses some of the results of a survey conducted a number of years ago to detect the impact of the New York State minimum-wage law. He states:

> A survey conducted by the New York Department of Labor showed that firms do reduce their benefits. The survey also indicated some of the benefits that undergo reduction. After

[21] Linda Leighton and Jacob Mincer, "The Effects of Minimum Wages on Human Capital Formation," in Simon Rottenberg, ed., *The Economics of Legal Minimum Wages* (Washington, D.C.: American Enterprise Institute, 1981).

44

the New York Retail Order of 1957 raised the minimum wage in retail stores, employers were asked if they had made any adjustments in their employee benefits since the minimum wage was increased. Of the 23,200 stores affected by the order, 714 stores reduced their hours of work, 597 reduced their 10-hour premiums (paid for spreading the work day over 10 hours), 429 reduced their daily-guarantee premium (a minimum guaranteed daily pay), 192 shortened rest and meal breaks, and 136 reduced such items as year-end bonuses, paid vacations, sick leave, and store-discount privileges. In addition, many stores reduced their work forces while others instituted a policy of not hiring extras during peak load seasons. In all likelihood, both of the latter changes increased the workloads of the remaining employees.[22]

Particularly noteworthy is the finding that evidently one of the principal ways by which employers respond to an increased minimum wage is to reduce hours of work. It is quite possible that the hours of work reduced are largely the hours that would otherwise be devoted to on-the-job training and that, as a result, the shortened hours become concentrated on performing job duties with less learning content than before.

The survey result just discussed is consistent with Gramlich's evidence, cited in chapter 1. He finds that for teenage labor, the employers tend to substitute part-time for full-time jobs. Such a substitution may partly reflect the employers' attempt to reduce the time spent by the workers on acquiring OJT.

Evidence appears compelling that minimum-wage legislation reduces on-the-job training for young workers. By forcing employers to pay increased current wages, the law deprives young workers of the opportunity to buy OJT by paying for it in reduced wages. At first sight, it might appear that the effect is simply to induce a substitution—a current wage increase rather than the future wage increases that OJT brings about. Economic logic suggests, however, that such forced substitution must necessarily reduce the combined well-being of the employer and the worker. This reduction is implied by the fact that the combined well-being is maximized at the free market equilibrium (see chapter 3). To be sure, it is possible in principle for

[22] Walter Wessels, "The Effect of Minimum Wages in the Presence of Fringe Benefits: An Expanded Model," *Economic Inquiry*, vol. 18, no. 2 (April 1980), pp. 293-313, at pp. 309-10. Lazear is currently investigating minimum-wage effects on wage growth of young workers. No written material on his findings is available at this writing.

workers to gain at the expense of the employers, but our evidence suggests that such a transfer did not occur for the period studied.

Reduction in human capital formation is obviously a serious public policy concern. It is pertinent to note, however, that minimum wages may encourage school attendance and thereby encourage the formation of human capital. There are two basic reasons to expect such effects. First, to the extent that minimum wages reduce the value of labor-market activity, either through direct unemployment or through the reduction in the full wage, they lower the opportunity cost of time devoted to formal schooling. Second, for a low-skilled worker, whose productivity merits him only a wage below the minimum wage, schooling is an obvious way of overcoming this handicap. Since minimum wages prohibit the worker from bidding for the right to a job at a lower wage, formal schooling then becomes an attractive investment as a way of raising his skill level.

The evidence on schooling effects has begun to appear only recently, and what is available is somewhat mixed. In my sample, which consists of those who were not enrolled in 1966 or in 1969, there is no evidence that some individuals went back to school in the interim years in response to the minimum wage. This finding must be interpreted with caution, however, because by examining only those who were not enrolled in either 1966 or 1969, I may have selected mostly those with above average distaste for attending school. Let us briefly examine the main results of three recent studies on this subject.

Ehrenberg and Marcus hypothesize that in response to an increased minimum wage, teenagers from poor families are likely to reduce their schooling and those from high-income families are likely to increase it.[23] The basic argument is that those from poor families are more likely than others to have to support themselves by working while in school. To the extent that minimum wages reduce these workers' employment opportunities—their primary method of financing schooling—they are unable to continue schooling. Children from nonpoor families have other sources of financing, and given the decreased opportunity cost and increased returns to schooling, they are induced to stay in school. If these effects are real, they argue, the minimum-wage law has the effect of perpetuating income inequality through its differential effects on educational attainment across socioeconomic groups, favoring children of nonpoor families.

The empirical findings of the Ehrenberg-Marcus study are somewhat mixed. In the 1970 census data for white teenagers, they find

[23] Ehrenberg and Marcus, "Minimum Wage Legislation."

the main effect of an increased minimum wage to be a redistribution of jobs from children of the poor to children of the nonpoor, without altering either group's enrollment outcomes. In the 1966 NLS data—the same data used for this study—an increased minimum wage for white male teenagers causes a shift from enrolled-employed to enrolled–not employed status for high-income children, but for low-income children the shift is from enrolled–part-time employment to not enrolled–full-time employment status, that is, a reduction in school enrollment. For nonwhites, their evidence is ambiguous. For those from high-income families, minimum wages appear to have no effect on the enrollment-employment outcomes, but for those from low-income families, the effect, as expected, is to induce a shift from full-time schooling to full-time employment, or a reduction in school enrollment. By and large their findings offer some support for the argument that minimum wages increase school attendance for nonpoor children but reduce it for poor children, though the evidence is far from being conclusive.

In the second study, James Cunningham reports evidence that tends to contradict the findings of Ehrenberg and Marcus.[24] Using the 1960 and 1970 census data, he finds that minimum wages tend to reduce school attendance of white teenagers of both sexes. The reduced school attendance appears to coincide with reduced employment opportunities for students. In contrast, black male teenagers tend to extend their schooling while working part-time or not working at all. He also finds a positive enrollment effect among black teenage females. Since Cunningham does not measure enrollment effects by income class, his evidence is not directly comparable with the evidence of Ehrenberg and Marcus. Nevertheless, the two studies report much conflicting evidence. Most notably, Cunningham's findings of positive enrollment effects for black teenagers are in sharp conflict with the negative enrollment effects reported by Ehrenberg and Marcus. I am unable to offer an explanation for the contradictory evidence.

Both the study of Ehrenberg and Marcus and that of Cunningham use cross-sectional data. Mattila examines time series data to test the hypothesis that minimum wages affect school enrollment.[25] His data are from the Current Population Survey and cover the years

[24] James Cunningham, "The Impact of Minimum Wages on Youth Employment, Hours of Work, and School Attendance: Cross-sectional Evidence from the 1960 and 1970 Censuses," in Rottenberg, *Economics of Legal Minimum Wages.*

[25] J. Peter Mattila, "The Impact of Minimum Wages on Teenage Schooling and on the Part-Time/Full-Time Employment of Youths," in Rottenberg, *Economics of Legal Minimum Wages.*

TABLE 4

EFFECT OF A 10 PERCENT INCREASE IN THE MINIMUM WAGE ON THE
PROPORTION OF TEENAGERS IN ENROLLMENT–LABOR
FORCE CATEGORIES

	14–17 Years		18–19 Years	
	Males	Females	Males	Females
1 Enrolled	0.0076[a]	0.0069[a]	0.0133[b]	0.0126[a]
a. In labor force	0.0091[b]	0.0072[b]	0.0077[b]	0.0077[b]
b. Out of labor force	0.0016	0.0032	0.0061	0.0036
2 Not enrolled	−0.0076[a]	−0.0069[a]	−0.0133[a]	−0.0126[a]
a. In labor force	−0.0069[a]	−0.0051[a]	−0.0112[b]	−0.0082[b]
b. Out of labor force	−0.0003	−0.0015	−0.0018	−0.0046

[a] Significant at 1 percent level.
[b] Significant at 5 percent level.
SOURCE: Abstracted from Mattila, "The Impact of Minimum Wages," table 4.

between 1947 and 1977, allowing him to capture the effect of nine
general increases in the minimum wage as well as the major expansions of coverage that went into effect in 1961, 1967, and 1974. Unfortunately his data do not distinguish between white and nonwhite
individuals or between income groups. His main findings are sum-
marized in table 4. The positive coefficients indicate that an increased
minimum wage results in an increased school enrollment in each
category.

Mattila's findings are the least ambiguous of the three studies
just cited. The evidence in the table clearly indicates that an increased
minimum wage increases the proportion of the population in school-
enrollment categories. What is most notable is the fact that the
increased enrollment effect reported in row 1 is so similar in magnitude
to the decreased not-enrolled labor force category reported in row 2a.
This finding suggests that the predominant response of teenagers to
the loss of employment opportunities caused by the minimum wage is
to stay in school if they are already enrolled and to enroll if they are
not enrolled, rather than to switch to other nonlabor activities.

Although the available evidence appears far from definitive,
the general indication is that minimum wages may increase school
enrollment of some youth groups. Clearly, any increase in school

enrollment tends to offset the adverse minimum-wage effects on human capital formation caused by the decreased on-the-job training. Is it possible, then, for the minimum-wage legislation to have the net effect of increasing the social welfare derived from human capital? The answer to this question is uncertain. Suppose that the human capital produced by either schooling or on-the-job training is largely a private good without external effects—effects falling on the society in addition to the effects felt by the individual decision makers—so that the magnitudes of costs and benefits perceived by individuals reflect fully their corresponding social magnitudes. In this case, elementary economics tells us that a free, competitive market based on voluntary exchange is efficient and enables the society to achieve the highest possible social welfare obtainable from available resources. An imposition of a minimum wage in such a market forces the economy away from the efficient solution and necessarily reduces the social welfare.

According to this economic reasoning, the minimum-wage legislation, by shifting the formation of human capital from OJT to schooling, enhances the social welfare only when such a shift generates a net increase of external benefits that is greater than the loss in private well-being. Put another way, if the free market were to lead to too little school-produced human capital and too much job-produced human capital, the minimum-wage law would help correct this imbalance. We have no way of knowing if that is the case in reality. If it were the case, however, a sound approach would be to choose among a variety of corrective policy alternatives. Although the minimum-wage law strikes me as a rather indirect way of dealing with the imbalance, it would be one of the available policy options. I am not aware of any argument favoring minimum wages as a means of encouraging school attendance, however.

Finally, I return to the issue with which this monograph began: the effects of the minimum wage on employment, unemployment, and labor force participation. My theoretical discussion implies that a decrease in the full wage leads to job changes and therefore may contribute to temporary increases in the time spent in unemployment and out of the labor force. To detect these effects, I ran additional regressions, using the same NLS data used earlier. Table 5 reports coefficients of the minimum-wage variable using the number of weeks unemployed and the number of weeks out of the labor force as the dependent variable. The complete regression results appear in appendix F. The term "young adults" refers here to individuals more than twenty years of age. The teen–young adult distinction cannot be used for 1968 and

TABLE 5
Minimum-Wage Effects on Weeks Unemployed and Weeks Out of Labor Force

Group	1967	1968	1969
Regressions of weeks unemployed			
White teens	−0.340 (−0.29)		
		0.398 (0.43)	−0.688 (−0.68)
White youths	0.176 (0.17)		
Black teens	2.690 (2.52)		
		1.027 (1.40)	0.203 (0.24)
Black youths	1.170 (1.33)		
Regressions of weeks out of labor force			
White teens	1.466 (0.72)		
		0.693 (0.46)	−4.597 (−2.63)
White youths	−0.932 (−0.51)		
Black teens	5.220 (2.86)		
		−0.163 (0.14)	−0.536 (0.38)
Black youths	−0.425 (−0.28)		

NOTE: The numbers are the regression coefficients (with *t*-values in parentheses) of the minimum-wage variable.
SOURCE: Appendix F.

1969, because by those years most individuals in our sample had reached twenty years of age.

The overall findings are rather ambiguous as to minimum-wage effects on the time spent unemployed and out of the labor force. I do find statistically significant adverse effects on the weeks of unemployment and the weeks out of the labor force for black teens, especially in 1967. Coefficients for whites are mostly statistically insignificant, however. It is not surprising to find adverse effects concentrated in the first year of minimum-wage changes. Such changes are well known in advance, and any adjustments to such changes tend to be made in earlier years. At any rate, discernible adverse effects on black unemployment and activities not associated with the labor market, along with ambiguous findings for whites, contrast sharply with the earlier ambiguous results for OJT effects on blacks.

5
Summary and Policy Alternatives

On-the-job training refers to opportunities that jobs offer a worker—both through a formal training program and through an informal setting—to acquire new skills, improve on the old, and gain knowledge conducive to increasing his productivity. These opportunities are of vital importance to young workers, for they help these workers gain a foothold in the world of work. Chapter 2 discusses how OJT and earnings are theoretically related and presents some evidence attesting to the validity of the theory.

An effective minimum wage diminishes these opportunities in two ways. First, to the extent that the minimum wage results in lost employment, it obviously deprives the disemployed worker of access to OJT. Such an outcome is a definite, if hidden, side effect of increased unemployment caused by the minimum wage. The literature reports a variety of evidence pointing to the minimum-wage law as a factor leading to high unemployment among young workers.[1] Some workers are fortunate enough to remain employed after an increase in the minimum wage. Even those workers who manage to remain employed at wages near the minimum wage may experience a reduction in OJT. This latter effect is the primary focus of this study. Chapter 3 presents a theory of why such a reduction may occur as the minimum wage is increased. For many young workers, who lack skills and experience, a legal minimum wage is likely to be higher than the wage they would earn otherwise. As a result, they are particularly susceptible to the adverse OJT effect of the minimum wage. The possibility that minimum-wage legislation will deprive these young workers of opportunities for OJT, and thereby condemn them to dead-end jobs, is of grave policy concern.

[1] See the first section of chapter 1.

My empirical research, which chapter 4 reports, has produced findings confirming the existence of such adverse effects of minimum wages. Because of the high reliability of the data for young white males, the findings for this group of workers constitute the most solid evidence supporting the underlying hypothesis of this study. Unfortunately, my findings for young black males are inconclusive because the data are unreliable. The data set for young blacks, for example, does not even confirm that accumulated work experience has a positive effect on earnings. Taken at face value, my estimates suggest that the 1967 revisions in the minimum-wage law reduced the value of OJT for young white males by some 26 to 31 percent, reflected as reduced earning power in 1969.

None of this is to suggest, however, that the minimum-wage legislation confers no benefit on young workers. One obvious benefit accrues in increased wages for the employed workers. But even though an increased minimum wage will increase the current wage for some workers, such a benefit, according to my evidence, is far smaller than the loss of future earnings caused by diminished OJT. Evidently, the minimum-wage legislation forces young workers to bargain away much of their future earnings for a small increase in current wage, to the deteriment of their economic well-being.

I hasten to remind the reader that the ambiguities associated with the black data prevented me from estimating the magnitude of the effects for blacks. For young white males, the evidence is quite compelling. Adverse minimum-wage effects are unmistakably there. It is worth noting that other recent studies discussed in chapter 4 corroborate this finding. In particular, the study by Leighton and Mincer clearly confirms the negative minimum-wage effects on OJT. Their evidence, like mine, is more definitive for whites than for blacks. On balance, the available evidence indicates that the minimum-wage legislation discourages human capital formation through OJT among young workers.

To be sure, the minimum wage may encourage school enrollments, and increased school enrollments tend to compensate for the lost human capital formation caused by the diminished OJT. As I argue in chapter 4, however, unless schooling produces greater external benefits than OJT, the forced shift of human capital from OJT to schooling will not lead to a net increase in the society's economic well-being. Even if schooling were found to have more externalities than OJT, it is by no means clear that an indirect policy like the minimum wage is the best policy instrument to effect the shift of resources from OJT to schooling. A much more direct way to encourage schooling is some form of subsidy to eligible youths.

Although the primary purpose of this study is to present a theoretical argument and an empirical analysis of the minimum-wage effects on OJT, I wish to discuss briefly some policy alternatives to the minimum wage. The most direct way to remove the barriers to OJT created by the minimum-wage legislation is to exempt young workers from the coverage. Such an exemption would apply at least to teenagers, if not to all youths up to twenty-four years of age. There have been many discussions of youth differentials, sometimes called teenage differentials, as a way of reducing the undesirable unemployment effects on youths.[2] Youth exemption would go further than a mere youth differential in eliminating adverse minimum-wage effects on both OJT and employment. It would eliminate the necessity to engage in endless debate about what the appropriate differential would be. Any differential chosen would be largely arbitrary anyway.

Exempting youths from minimum-wage coverage may raise the specter of youth poverty. Such a conclusion presumes in the first place, however, that the minimum-wage legislation is an effective antipoverty device. Above and beyond the adverse side effects, the minimum-wage law is by now well recognized as an ineffective instrument for reducing poverty. Its main deficiency is that it raises wages for all low-wage workers, regardless of family income.[3] Surely the accumulating evidence on its harmful effects on OJT as well as on current employment opportunities renders the case for the minimum wage as an antipoverty device the weakest when applied to youths. If youth poverty is the issue, what is needed is a sound income maintenance program, which would transfer income to poor youths efficiently.

Transfer of income cannot take place without impairing incentives. The problem is to devise a policy of helping the poor with the minimum impairment of incentives. In this regard, a sound antipoverty policy for youths is no different from suitable policy for poverty in general. A negative income tax, for example, has been discussed extensively as an attractive alternative by economists and others concerned with antipoverty policies.[4] It is seldom acknowledged

[2] See, for example, Finis Welch, *Minimum Wages: Issues and Evidence* (Washington, D.C.: American Enterprise Institute, 1978), pp. 42-45.

[3] According to Gramlich, in 1973 fully 40 percent of low-wage-earning teenagers were in families with incomes above $15,000. See Edward M. Gramlich, "Impact of Minimum Wages on Other Wages, Employment, and Family Incomes," *Brookings Papers on Economic Activity*, no. 2 (Washington, D.C., 1976), p. 445.

[4] This is not the place to elaborate on the details of the negative income tax. A simple illustration may be useful, however. The simplest scheme may be characterized by the following formula: Take-Home Pay = (1 − Tax Rate) × (Earnings

that George J. Stigler as early as 1946 suggested such a scheme as a policy alternative to the minimum wage in his classic article on the minimum wage.[5] I wish to reemphasize the attractiveness of a negative income tax as an alternative to the minimum wage. A negative income tax can be implemented with a minimum of administrative machinery, and its parameters can be chosen to reflect family size, composition, etc., in order to determine the level of need for income transfer. Ideally, the whole minimum-wage law would be replaced by a more effective antipoverty policy, such as the negative income tax.

In view of the vested interest groups that the current welfare programs have spawned, however, an economywide implementation of a negative income tax program may take time. Its implementation for youths alone, together with the youth exemption from the minimum-wage law, would be a good start. Youth exemption coupled with a negative income tax program would eliminate the undesirable side effects of the minimum wage discussed in this monograph while at the same time reducing poverty among young workers.

It is quite possible, however, that the resistance to youth exemption, or even to youth differentials, would turn out to be politically insurmountable. The literature is slowly accumulating on why the minimum-wage legislation has gained such wide support despite economists' persistent warnings about its defects.[6] If the minimum-

---

before Tax) + Guaranteed Income. Suppose the program specifies the tax rate to be 0.20 (20 percent flat rate) and the guaranteed income to be $2,000. Then the reader may easily verify that with earnings before tax of less than $10,000— the break-even income—the take-home pay is *larger* than the earnings. In other words, there is a subsidy, or a negative tax, on earnings below the break-even income. An important point, however, is that the take-home pay increases with earnings, a feature that encourages working. Above the break-even income, there is a regular positive tax and the take-home pay is less than the earnings. Obviously both the tax rate and the guaranteed income are the policy parameters, the choice of which will help control program costs, including the disincentive effects. See Albert Rees and Harold W. Watts, "An Overview of the Labor Supply Results," in J. A. Pechman and P. M. Timpane, eds., *Work Incentives and Income Guarantees* (Washington, D.C.: Brookings Institution, 1975), for related discussions.

[5] George J. Stigler, "The Economics of Minimum Wage Legislation," *American Economic Review*, vol. 36 (June 1946), pp. 358-65.

[6] That those representing the interests of northern industrial states tend to support minimum wages more vigorously than those from southern states was explained by Henry Simon in terms of northerners' desire to eliminate southern comparative advantage in labor costs. See Henry C. Simon. *Economic Policy for a Free Society* (Chicago: University of Chicago Press, 1948), pp. 135-38. See also Jonathan I. Silberman and Garey C. Durden, "Determining Legislative Preferences on the Minimum Wage: An Economic Approach," *Journal of Political Economy*, vol. 84, no. 2 (April 1976), pp. 317-29. The motive of trade unions for

wage legislation must remain on the books, some form of subsidy to encourage the formation of human capital may be called for. Martin Feldstein proposes a youth employment scholarship, which would be paid to young workers as a supplement to their wage income.[7] The major attraction of this program, unlike a subsidy or a tax credit given to the employer, is that it relies on the individual youth to choose the job that gives him the most valuable combination of training and current wage. Thus it allows individual differences in interests, time preferences, and abilities their full play in determining the optimum combination of training and current wage.

Feldstein proposes the subsidy program as a way of encouraging OJT. To promote an efficient use of such a subsidy in the formation of human capital, however, the subsidy should be made applicable either to training on the job or to training at school. For example, an eligible youth might receive a voucher entitling him to a certain amount of training, and he might use it at work or at a vocational school, a community college, or even a four-year college. Either the employer or the school selected by the youth would then redeem the voucher for cash. Since schools are already subsidized and OJT is not, the voucher would not be made transferable between OJT and schooling on a dollar-by-dollar basis. Instead, an appropriate rate of transfer would have to be established to reflect the already existing imbalance in the subsidy. The point is simply that by making the voucher applicable to either source of training, the subsidy program would avoid distorting resource allocation between OJT and schooling. It would help promote competition among employers and among schools, as well as between employers and schooling, in offering training services of quality.[8]

There may be many other reasonable policy alternatives. It is not my intention to present a complete catalog of possible policies to deal with the undesirable side effects of the minimum-wage legislation, nor do I wish to prescribe a particular policy instrument. Details of each policy surely require much more attention than the

---

their vigorous support of the minimum-wage legislation is obvious and is frequently discussed in elementary textbooks. Recently Leffler argued, and presented some evidence in support of his argument, that poverty-group representatives support the minimum-wage law because the law reduces the cost of establishing eligibility for the increasingly generous public assistance programs. Keith B. Leffler, "Minimum Wages, Welfare, and Wealth Transfers to the Poor," *Journal of Law and Economics*, vol. 21 (October 1978), pp. 345-58.

[7] Martin Feldstein, "The Economics of the New Unemployment," *Public Interest*, vol. 33 (Fall 1973), pp. 16-17.

[8] The idea of the educational voucher is discussed by Milton Friedman in *Capitalism and Freedom* (Chicago: University of Chicago Press, 1962).

discussion here has offered before one could rank them by their attractiveness. I simply wish to urge that serious and informed policy discussions are now called for to address particularly the harmful effects of minimum wages on young workers. The two policies offered above, the voucher for youth training and youth exemptions coupled with a negative income tax, possess attractive features for rectifying the damage the minimum-wage law inflicts on youths.

Appendix A

Algebraic Formulation of Aspects
of the Model

This appendix presents an algebraic sketch of some crucial aspects of the model.[1]

Competitive Equilibrium in the Absence of Minimum Wages

Let the demand and supply curves be given by:

$$W^d = a(T) + b(T) E$$
$$W^s = m - T + nE \qquad \text{(A-1)}$$

where W^d is the pecuniary wage offer, T is the amount of OJT per man, E is employment, W^s is the pecuniary asking wage, and m and n are constants. Both a and b are functions of T. The demand and supply curves are characterized by the following restrictions:

$$a(0) > m, \, da/dT < 0, \, d^2a/dT^2 < 0$$
$$m,n > 0, \, b < 0, \, db/dT \gtreqless 0 \qquad \text{(A-2)}$$

Let E_0 denote the levels of employment at the intersections of the demand and supply curves. That is:

$$a + bE_0 = m - T + nE_0$$

or

$$E_0 = \frac{m - T - a}{b - n} \qquad \text{(A-3)}$$

This is the equation for the wage-employment locus depicted in figures 5 and 6.

[1] For further details, see Masanori Hashimoto, "Minimum Wage and Earnings Growth of Young Male Workers," manuscript, University of Washington, 1981.

Let K denote the sum of the gains accruing to the consumers and to the producers, that is, the gains from exchange; using equations A–1 and A–3, one obtains K as:

$$K \equiv \int_0^{E_0} (W^d - W^s)\, dE = \frac{1}{2} \frac{(a - m + T)^2}{n - b} \qquad \text{(A–4)}$$

To examine the properties of the competitive equilibrium, maximize K with respect to T. The first-order condition for the maximum is given by:

$$-\frac{da}{dT} - \frac{1}{2} \frac{(a - m + T)}{n - b} \frac{db}{dT} = 1 \qquad \text{(A–5)}$$
$$\underset{(-)}{} \qquad \underset{(+)}{} \qquad \underset{(?)}{}$$

Thus in competitive equilibrium the marginal cost of OJT in the left side of equation A–5 is equated to the marginal value, which is one dollar by definition in the right side of the equation.

I now show that the maximum gains solution is equivalent to the maximum employment solution if and only if the demand curves are parallel to one another. Using equation A–3, maximize E_0 with respect to T to obtain the first-order condition as follows:

$$-\frac{da}{dT} - \frac{(a - m + T)}{n - b} \frac{db}{dT} = 1 \qquad \text{(A–6)}$$
$$\underset{(-)}{} \qquad \underset{(+)}{} \qquad \underset{(?)}{}$$

Comparing equations A–5 and A–6, one sees that the two are equivalent to each other if and only if $db/dT = 0$. Put another way, only when the demand curves are parallel to one another is the competitive solution equivalent to the maximum employment solution. In general, the competitive equilibrium does not maximize employment. Recall now that $-da/dT$ is specified in equation A–2 to be a monotonically increasing function of T. Therefore, according to equations A–5 and A–6, the amount of OJT at the competitive equilibrium is smaller or larger than at the maximum employment point, depending on whether $db/dT \gtreqless 0$. The case discussed in chapter 3 and in figure 7 implies that $db/dT < 0$. The competitive equilibrium (C in figure 7) occurs below the maximum employment point on the wage-employment locus (equation A–3). Clearly the equilibrium amount of OJT is larger than the amount at the maximum employment point. In this case, a minimum wage may increase employment, though it unambiguously decreases OJT. If $db/dT > 0$, however, the competitive equilibrium occurs above the maximum employment point on the wage-employment locus. In this case, the minimum wage decreases both employment and OJT.

Effects of the Minimum Wage on the Noncovered Sector

Assume that the covered and the noncovered sectors start out with identical demand and supply conditions. The introduction of the minimum wage shifts the supply curves in the noncovered sector. The noncovered sector is characterized as follows:

$$W^d = a(T) + b(T) E$$

$$W^s = m - x - T + nE \tag{A-7}$$

where accordingly as $x \gtreqless 0$, there is an inflow of workers to, or an outflow from, this sector. The wage-employment locus is given by:

$$E_0 = \frac{a - m + x + T}{n - b} \tag{A-8}$$

and the sum of the gains is given by:

$$K \equiv \int_0^{E_0} (W^d - W^s) \, dE = \frac{1}{2} \frac{(a - m + x + T)^2}{n - b} \tag{A-9}$$

The first-order condition for maximizing K with respect to T is given by:

$$-\frac{da}{dT} - \frac{(a - m + T + x)}{2(n - b)} \frac{db}{dT} = 1 \tag{A-10}$$

If the demand curves are parallel to one another, the first-order condition is reduced to $-da/dT = 1$. Since x does not appear in this condition, the minimum wage does not affect the amount of OJT in the noncovered sector. In general, the demand curves are not parallel to one another, and the minimum-wage effects on OJT depend on the sign of db/dT as well as on whether the minimum wage causes an inflow to or an outflow from this sector. If db/dT is positive (negative), the equilibrium magnitude of $-da/dT$, and therefore the amount of OJT, is larger (smaller) if there is an inflow ($x > 0$) than if there is an outflow of workers.

Appendix B

The Minimum-Wage Index

The minimum-wage index (M) is a geometric average over the three years of the yearly minimum-wage index (M_j), where $j = 1967, 1968,$ and 1969. M_j is assigned to each individual by adopting the following formula:

$$M_j = \frac{MB_j}{\hat{W}_j}(C_{1j}D_{1j} + C_{2j}D_{2j} + \ldots) + \frac{MN_j}{\hat{W}_j}(C'_{1j}D'_{1j} + C'_{2j}D'_{2j} + \ldots)$$

The term MB_j is the basic nominal minimum wage, which increased from \$1.25 to \$1.40 in February 1967 and then to \$1.60 after February 1968, and MN_j is the nominal minimum wage applicable to newly covered sectors, which was \$1.00 after February 1967, \$1.15 after February 1968, \$1.30 after February 1969, and \$1.45 after February 1970, finally becoming equal to the basic minimum wage of \$1.60 in February 1971. The coefficients C_{ij} are the proportion of employment covered by the basic minimum wage in each industry, and those designated C'_{ij} are the proportion of employment covered by the newly applicable minimum in each industry. The dummy variables D_{ij} and D'_{ij} indicate the worker's industrial attachment. If he works in the ith industry, the values of D_{ij} and D'_{ij} are both unity. The term $\hat{W}_j$ is the estimate of what the individual's wage rate would have been in year j in the absence of changes in the minimum-wage law. It is calculated from an earnings function similar to the one developed by Mincer[1] and estimated by using relevant information for 1966, one year before the change in the minimum-wage law. The earnings function relates the logarithm of the 1966 hourly wage rate to schooling, years of work experience, a black-white dummy variable, a North-

[1] Jacob Mincer, *Schooling, Experience, and Earnings* (New York: National Bureau of Economic Research, 1974).

South dummy variable, and a set of twelve industrial variables. The estimated earnings function is then used to predict wage rates in each year between 1967 and 1969. In calculating the predicted wage rates, we adjust the coefficients for the industrial dummy variables by the industry-specific growth rate of average earnings since 1966 to allow for the secular trend in the wage rate. The mean and the standard deviations of M are 0.51 and 0.18, respectively.

Appendix C

Regression Estimates for Table 3

Table 6 presents the regression estimates of $(\ln W_{69} - \ln W_{66})$ used for table 3.

TABLE 6

Regressions of $(\ln W_{69} - \ln W_{66})$

Explanatory Variable	Regression Number			
	1	2	3	4
Constant	−2.492	2.936	−1.329	1.376
	(−2.45)	(1.74)	(−2.55)	(2.00)
ΔE	1.025	−0.698	0.573	−0.050
	(2.98)	(−1.17)	(3.52)	(−0.24)
S_0	0.056	0.033	0.051	0.069
	(2.18)	(0.68)	(2.27)	(2.15)
EXP_0	0.029	0.013	0.028	0.058
	(1.44)	(0.30)	(1.55)	(1.85)
AGE_0	−0.032	−0.034	−0.035	−0.085
	(−1.55)	(−0.74)	(−1.90)	(−2.49)
M	3.269	−1.090	2.250	−0.079
	(3.14)	(−0.90)	(2.50)	(−0.93)
$MX\Delta E$	−1.020	0.388	−0.624	0.066
	(−2.81)	(0.88)	(−2.00)	(0.21)
$UNX\Delta E$	−0.156	−0.166	−0.601	f.o.
	(−1.20)	(−1.29)	(−3.63)	
$\Delta SX\Delta E$	−0.164	−0.188	−0.210	−0.584
	(−2.08)	(−0.61)	(−2.61)	(−2.02)
$\hat{W}X\Delta E$	−0.130	0.189	—	—
	(−1.40)	(1.03)		

TABLE 6   (continued)

Explanatory Variable	Regression Number			
	1	2	3	4
ΔH	−0.002	−0.003	−0.003	−0.002
	(−1.63)	(−1.13)	(−1.99)	(−0.80)
MR_0	−0.066	0.030	−0.068	−0.002
	(−2.33)	(0.52)	(−2.40)	(−0.32)
$\hat{W}$	0.294	−0.674	—	—
	(1.09)	(−1.31)		
ΔS	0.462	0.680	0.578	1.731
	(2.27)	(0.87)	(2.77)	(2.42)
UN	0.498	0.567	1.764	0.061
	(1.33)	(1.60)	(3.71)	(1.11)
DUM	—	—	−0.282	0.012
			(−2.26)	(0.14)
$DUMX\Delta E$	—	—	−0.001	−0.0005
			(−2.76)	(−1.23)
$\bar{R}^2$	0.064	0.056	0.073	0.050
SEE	0.323	0.354	0.323	0.355
Sample size	651	197	661	226

NOTE: — = not included; f.o. = variables forced out because of multicollinearity; t-values appear in parentheses.

SOURCE: National Longitudinal Survey (NLS): Young Males, 1966-69; see chapter 4 for variable definitions.

Appendix D

Means of Variables for Table 3

Table 7 shows the means and standard deviations of the explanatory variables in table 3.

TABLE 7

MEANS OF RELEVANT EXPLANATORY VARIABLES FOR TABLE 3

| | For Regressions: | | For Regressions: | |
Explanatory Variable	1 Whites	2 Blacks	3 Whites	4 Blacks
M	0.446	0.676	0.449	0.671
	(0.125)	(0.174)	(0.139)	(0.190)
UN	0.305	0.335	0.304	0.292
	(0.461)	(0.473)	(0.460)	(0.455)
ΔS (years)	0.039	0.024	0.038	0.021
	(0.245)	(0.154)	(0.243)	(0.143)
$\hat{W}$ ($)	2.758	1.928	2.739	1.823
	(0.480)	(0.426)	(0.506)	(0.485)
DUM	—	—	0.014	0.142
			(0.118)	(0.349)

NOTE: Standard deviations appear in parentheses.
SOURCE: The same as for appendix C.

Appendix E

Elasticities of OJT and the Full Wage

The definition of OJT is given by:

$$OJT \equiv \frac{dW_t}{d\Delta E} D = W_t \frac{d\ln W_t}{d\Delta E} D \qquad \text{(E–1)}$$

where D is the present value of a stream of one dollar accruing every year from now until retirement. Therefore, the elasticity of OJT with respect to M is given by:

$$\eta_{OJT} = \eta_{W_t} + \eta_V \qquad \text{(E–2)}$$

where η denotes elasticities with respect to M, W_t stands for pecuniary wage, and $V \equiv d\ln W_t / d\Delta E$. From equation 6, the elasticity of the full wage is seen to be a weighted average of the elasticities of W_t and OJT, the weight being the proportion of each component in the full wage. That is:

$$\eta_F = P_{W_t}\eta_{W_t} + (1 - P_{W_t})\eta_{OJT} \qquad \text{(E–3)}$$

where P_{W_t} equals W_t/F. According to my estimates based on regression 3, for whites only, η_{W_t} and η_V evaluated at the means of the relevant variables are, respectively, 0.21 and -2.76, so that η_{OJT} equals -2.54. Since P_{W_t} turns out to equal 0.50 in this regression, η_F is calculated to be -1.17 [= $0.50(0.21) + 0.50(-2.54)$].

Appendix F

Regressions of Weeks Unemployed and Weeks Out of Labor Force

Regressions of weeks unemployed and weeks out of the labor force are shown in table 8 for 1967 and in table 9 for 1968 and 1969.

TABLE 8

REGRESSIONS OF WEEKS UNEMPLOYED AND WEEKS OUT OF LABOR FORCE, 1967

	Weeks Unemployed	Weeks Out of Labor Force
Minimum-wage index		
White teens (15–19)	−0.340 (−0.29)	1.466 (0.72)
Black teens	2.690 (2.52)	5.220 (2.85)
White young adults (20–25)	0.176 (0.17)	−0.932 (−0.51)
Black young adults	1.170 (1.33)	−0.425 (−0.28)
Years of education	−0.249 (−2.21)	−0.254 (−1.31)
Years of work experience	−0.036 (−0.39)	−0.217 (−1.40)
Married in 1966 (dummy variable)	−1.073 (−3.40)	−1.568 (−2.91)
Living in central cities (dummy variable)	0.739 (2.26)	—
Region of residence (dummy variable)		
North	−0.167 (−0.38)	−0.035 (−0.05)
South	−0.968 (−2.26)	−0.456 (−0.62)
Mountain	−0.243 (−0.243)	−0.875 (−0.51)
West	1.069 (1.83)	−0.352 (−0.35)
Constant	4.701 (2.93)	7.132 (2.60)
$\bar{R}^2$	0.06	0.05
SEE	4.40	7.54
N	946	946

NOTE: The coefficient for region of residence refers to the difference between a particular region and the East. Numbers in parentheses are t-values.

SOURCE: National Longitudinal Survey: 1967.

TABLE 9

REGRESSIONS OF WEEKS UNEMPLOYED AND WEEKS OUT OF LABOR FORCE, 1968 AND 1969

	Weeks Unemployed		Weeks Out of Labor Force	
	1968	1969	1968	1969
Minimum-wage index				
Whites	0.398	−0.688	0.693	−4.597
	(0.43)	(−0.68)	(0.46)	(−2.63)
Blacks	1.425	0.203	−0.163	−0.536
	(1.40)	(0.24)	(0.14)	(0.38)
Years of education	−0.335	−0.313	−0.494	−0.286
	(−3.78)	(−3.93)	(−3.42)	(−2.09)
Years of experience	−0.132	−0.137	−0.239	−0.136
	(−2.10)	(−2.46)	(−2.32)	(−1.41)
Married (dummy variable)	−0.856	−1.102	−2.454	−1.950
	(−2.81)	(−3.89)	(−4.95)	(−3.99)
Living in central cities	0.022	−0.043	1.239	−0.092
	(−0.07)	(−0.15)	(2.46)	(−0.19)
Region of residence (dummy variable)				
North	0.471	−0.518	−0.887	0.324
	(1.16)	(−1.42)	(−1.34)	(0.51)
South	0.097	−0.501	−1.616	−0.330
	(0.24)	(−1.38)	(−2.44)	(−0.53)
Mountain	−0.018	0.208	−0.935	1.030
	(−0.02)	(0.25)	(−0.61)	(0.73)
West	0.993	0.073	0.580	0.496
	(1.86)	(0.15)	(0.67)	(0.59)
Constant	5.147	6.441	10.285	8.736
	(3.80)	(5.00)	(4.66)	(3.94)
$\bar{R}^2$	0.04	0.04	0.06	0.03
SEE	4.34	3.93	7.07	6.77
N	1,012	1,012	1,012	1,012

NOTE: The coefficient for region of residence refers to the difference between a particular region and the East. The distinction between teens and young adults could not be made for 1968 and 1969 because of the small number of teenagers. Numbers in parentheses are t-values.

SOURCE: National Longitudinal Survey: 1968, 1969.

Bibliography

Ashenfelter, Orley, and Smith, Robert. "Compliance with the Minimum Wage Law." *Journal of Political Economy* 87, no. 2 (April 1979): 333–50.

Barzel, Yoram. "Measurement Cost and the Economic Organization of Markets." Manuscript. University of Washington, 1980.

Becker, Gary S. "Investment in Human Capital: A Theoretical Analysis." *Journal of Political Economy* 70, supplement (October 1962): 9–49.

Ben-Porath, Yoram. "The Production of Human Capital and the Life Cycle of Earnings." *Journal of Political Economy* 75 (August 1967): 352–65.

Brown, Charles; Gilroy, Curtis; and Kohen, Andrew. *Effects of the Minimum Wage on Youth Employment and Unemployment.* Minimum Wage Study Commission Working Paper, no. 1. Washington, D.C., 1980.

Cunningham, James. "The Impact of Minimum Wages on Youth Employment, Hours of Work, and School Attendance: Cross-sectional Evidence from the 1960 and 1970 Censuses." In *The Economics of Legal Minimum Wages*, edited by Simon Rottenberg. Washington, D.C.: American Enterprise Institute, 1981.

Ehrenberg, Ronald G., and Marcus, Alan J. "Minimum Wage Legislation and the Educational Outcomes of Youths." *Research in Labor Economics.* In press.

Feldstein, Martin. "The Economics of the New Unemployment." *Public Interest* 33 (Fall 1973): 3–42.

Friedman, Milton. *Capitalism and Freedom.* Chicago: University of Chicago Press, 1962.

Ginzberg, Eli. "Youth Unemployment." *Scientific American* 242, no. 5 (May 1980): 43–49.

Goldfarb, Robert. "The Policy Content of Quantitative Minimum

Wage Research." *Industrial Relations Research Association Proceedings* (1974): 261–68.

Gramlich, Edward M. "Impact of Minimum Wages on Other Wages, Employment, and Family Incomes." *Brookings Papers on Economic Activity*, no. 2 (Washington, D.C., 1976): 409–61.

Grossman, Jonathan. "Fair Labor Standards Act of 1938: Maximum Struggle for a Minimum Wage." *Monthly Labor Review* 101 (June 1978): 22–30.

Hashimoto, Masanori. "Bonus Payments, On-the-Job Training and Lifetime Employment in Japan." *Journal of Political Economy* 87, no. 5 (October 1979): 1086–104.

———. "Firm-Specific Human Capital as a Shared Investment." *American Economic Review*. In press.

———. "Minimum Wage and Earnings Growth of Young Male Workers." Manuscript. University of Washington, 1981.

Hashimoto, Masanori, and Mincer, Jacob. "Employment and Unemployment Effects of Minimum Wages." Mimeographed. Washington, D.C.: National Bureau of Economic Research, 1970.

Kosters, Marvin, and Welch, Finis. "The Effects of Minimum Wages on the Distribution of Changes in Aggregate Employment." *American Economic Review* 62, no. 3 (June 1972): 323–32.

Kuratani, Masatoshi. "The Theory of Training, Earnings and Employment." Ph.D. diss., Columbia University, 1973.

Lazear, Edward. "Age, Experience, and Wage Growth." *American Economic Review* 66 (September 1976): 548–58.

———. "The Narrowing of Black-White Wage Differential Is Illusory." *American Economic Review* 69 (September 1979): 553–64.

Leffler, Keith B. "Minimum Wages, Welfare, and Wealth Transfers to the Poor." *Journal of Law and Economics* 21 (October 1978): 345–58.

Leighton, Linda, and Mincer, Jacob. "The Effects of Minimum Wages on Human Capital Formation." In *The Economics of Legal Minimum Wages*, edited by Simon Rottenberg. Washington, D.C.: American Enterprise Institute, 1981.

Mattila, J. Peter. "The Impact of Minimum Wages on Teenage Schooling and on the Part-Time/Full-Time Employment of Youths." In *The Economics of Legal Minimum Wages*, edited by Simon Rottenberg. Washington, D.C.: American Enterprise Institute, 1981.

Mincer, Jacob, "On-the-Job Training, Costs, Returns, and Some Implications." *Journal of Political Economy* 70, supplement (October 1962): 50–79.

———. *Schooling, Experience, and Earnings*. New York: National Bureau of Economic Research, 1974.

———. "Unemployment Effects of Minimum Wages." *Journal of Political Economy* 84, no. 4, part 2 (August 1976): S87–S104.

Mixon, Wilson. "Some Economic Effects of Minimum Wage Legislation." Ph.D. diss., University of Washington, 1974.

Moore, Thomas Gale. "The Effects of Minimum Wages on Teenage Unemployment Rates." *Journal of Political Economy* 79, no. 4 (July/August 1971): 897–902.

Oi, Walter W. "Labor as a Quasi-fixed Factor." *Journal of Political Economy* 70, no. 6 (December 1962): 538–55.

Parnes, Herbert S. "The National Longitudinal Surveys: New Vistas for Labor Market Research." *American Economic Review* 65, no. 2 (May 1975): 244–49.

Parsons, Donald O. "Models of Labor Market Turnover: A Theoretical and Empirical Survey." *Research in Labor Economics* 1 (1977): 185–223.

Ragan, James. "Minimum Wages and Youth Labor Market." *Review of Economics and Statistics* 59, no. 2 (May 1977): 129–36.

Rees, Albert, and Watts, Harold W. "An Overview of the Labor Supply Results." In *Work Incentives and Income Guarantees,* edited by Joseph A. Pechman and P. Michael Timpane. Washington, D.C.: Brookings Institution, 1975.

Rosen, Sherwin. "Learning and Experience in the Labor Market." *Journal of Human Resources* 7, no. 3 (Summer 1972): 326–42.

————. "Short-Run Employment Variations in Class-I Railroads in the United States." *Econometrica* 36 (July 1968): 511–29.

Scott, John Paul, ed. *Critical Periods.* Stroudsberg, Pa.: Dowden, Hutchinson and Ross, 1978.

Shabecoff, Phillip. "U.S. Finds Big Jobless Rate in Youth Ranks." *New York Times,* February 29, 1980.

Shimada, Haruo. "The Structure of Earnings and Investments in Human Resources: A Comparison between the United States and Japan. Ph.D. diss., University of Wisconsin—Madison, 1974.

Silberman, Jonathan I., and Durden, Garey C. "Determining Legislative Preferences on the Minimum Wage: An Economic Approach." *Journal of Political Economy* 84, no. 2 (April 1976): 317–29.

Simon, Henry C. *Economic Policy for a Free Society.* Chicago: University of Chicago Press, 1948.

Stigler, George J. "The Economics of Minimum Wage Legislation." *American Economic Review* 36 (June 1946): 358–65.

U.S. Congress. *U.S. Code: Congressional and Administrative News,* no. 3. 95th Congress, 1st session, 1977: 1245–53, 3201–61.

U.S. Department of Labor, Employment Standards Administration. *Minimum Wage and Maximum Hour Standards under the Fair Labor Standards Act.* Various years.

Welch, Finis. *Minimum Wages: Issues and Evidence.* Washington, D.C.: American Enterprise Institute, 1978.

————. "The Rising Impact of Minimum Wages." *Regulation* (November/December 1978): 28–37.

Wessels, Walter. "The Effect of Minimum Wages in the Presence of Fringe Benefits: An Expanded Model." *Economic Inquiry* 18, no. 2 (April 1980): 293–313.

A NOTE ON THE BOOK

The typeface used for the text of this book is
Palatino, designed by Hermann Zapf.
The type was set by
Hendricks-Miller Typographic Company, of Washington, D.C.
Thomson-Shore, Inc., of Dexter, Michigan, printed
and bound the book, using Warren's Olde Style paper.
The cover and format were designed by Pat Taylor,
and the figures were drawn by Hördur Karlsson.
The manuscript was edited by Marcia Brubeck and
by Gertrude Kaplan, of the AEI Publications staff.